LISTS TO LOVE BY
FOR BUSY WIVES

LISTS TO LOVE BY FOR BUSY WIVES

Simple Steps to the Marriage You Want

Mark and Susan Merrill

New York Boston Nashville

FaithWords
Hachette Book Group
1290 Avenue of the Americas, New York, NY 10104
faithwords.com
twitter.com/faithwords

First Edition: January 2017

FaithWords is a division of Hachette Book Group, Inc.
The FaithWords name and logo are trademarks of Hachette Book Group, Inc.

The publisher is not responsible for websites (or their content)
that are not owned by the publisher.

The Hachette Speakers Bureau provides a wide range of authors for speaking events. To find out more, go to www.hachettespeakersbureau.com or call (866) 376-6591.

Library of Congress Cataloging-in-Publication Data has been applied for.

ISBNs: 978-1-4555-9680-5 (hardcover), 978-1-4555-9681-2 (ebook)

Printed in the United States of America

LSC-C

10   9   8   7   6   5   4   3   2

To our daughters Megan, Emily and Hannah, and to every woman who desires to love her husband well

CONTENTS

Contents

Contents

INTRODUCTION

I can do everything. At least I thought I could when Mark and I got married. I have a creative, high-energy, and people-pleasing personality. So "doing" anything and everything was fun for me and rarely taxing. I liked to challenge myself to give 110 percent, and it became a personal game. Looking back, I think what I expected from myself and my marriage was inflated by the success I had pushing myself to creatively do more. I naturally applied this life experience to marriage. Certainly marriage would be the same or even easier to do well—no work involved. I thought the hard part was finding a husband, not living happily ever after. I assumed that happily ever after would just be a reality once I said, "I do." Ironically, I failed to realize that saying "I do" involved more "doing" than everything I had attempted to do in my life!

The first year of our marriage was easy. Mark was a lawyer and I was a banker, so our networks, friends, and interests were the same. When our first daughter arrived around our one-year anniversary, I quit my job to be a stay-at-home mom. Suddenly I was home without the outlet I needed to use my energy and creativity. So I started getting involved in everything I could. I got involved in Bible studies and church. I started a play group. We had more children. I volunteered at their schools. I volunteered for their coaches, teachers, and principals. I enjoyed every minute. I got to be with my kids at every school trip and team practice. I got to know their teachers and coaches and friends' parents. I was having a good time "doing" for my kids.

But I had left my "I do" to Mark behind. And Mark is very different from me. He doesn't have the same personality and didn't understand my need for those outlets.

Mark: *Susan was running around all over the place. While I thought she was neglecting me a bit, the main issue that I saw was that she was different from me. Unfortunately, I had a high view of myself back then and thought she needed to change. I felt like I was how a person should be. She should do things like me, talk like me, and think like me. So I set out to change her.*

Mark wanted me to stop doing many of the things I was doing. Looking back, I was definitely overcommitted and was taking him for granted. I had just assumed that Mark was my teammate in life and parenting. I didn't see him as a person who also needed my attention. At the same time I was feeling squashed. I would lie in bed at night, unable to sleep, ruminating about all the ideas of things I thought would be great to do.

Then Mark became rather critical of how I was and what I did. The people pleaser in me went into overdrive. One week he wanted me to change one thing and the next week it would be something new. He was like an ice cream shop. I called whatever he wanted me to do the flavor of the week, because it was always different from the last week but equally important. I would work on changing something, and then I would drop it because he wanted me to work on something else. I felt as if I couldn't do anything right. In the past, I had always found a way to please. Not now. I was still giving 110 percent, but this time it wasn't working. Marriage became hard work.

Mark: *The ironic thing is that Susan actually did start to change and become more like me, and when she did, I didn't like it. I missed the real her. The last thing our marriage needed was for us to be exactly like each other.*

I was taking Mark's needs for granted and he was trying to change me. I thought it would be easy, but building a great marriage for a lifetime takes work. An amazing bottle of wine doesn't just arrive on its own and neither does an amazing marriage. It is the result of years of care and cultivation. The smallest things can make a big difference. Falling in love happens, but marriage does *not* guarantee that you will stay in love forever. Love in marriage takes cultivation. Actually for some, like me, it takes a lot of cultivation!

But the effort can be rewarding if you can make small steps of progress that you can celebrate and feel good about.

Is it hard? Overwhelming? Complicated? It doesn't have to be—that is the purpose of this book. Each list gives you simple steps to the marriage you want. So how can you cultivate your love for your husband in a busy, demanding world? By working on it a little every day so that slowly, but surely, it grows with each passing day and year into the relationship you've always dreamed of.

In this book are lists that you can use to love your husband well. They will help you love him more deeply when you feel like it and when you don't feel like it; when the love in your marriage is a two-way street and when it's a one-way street. I want to acknowledge those of you who may be on the one-way street and affirm you for trying to love well when that love may not be reciprocated. The fact that you purchased this book in an effort to honor the covenant you made before God to love your husband will not go unnoticed by God. It is my hope that you will experience God's love when you are missing your husband's.

ABOUT THIS BOOK

You may be wondering how we came up with the concept of lists to love by and why we know they will work. For more than two decades we've been sharing marriage content. Our posts have received tens of millions of page views during that time.

A careful analysis of our Google Analytics reports, combined with our experiences over these years, tell us that there is a recurring theme with most of our high-ranking marriage content. Each post addresses one or all of the following common denominators: expectations, evaluation, or improvements. People are searching on Google for ways to manage their expectations, evaluate how they are doing, and improve their marriages. The lists in this book will help you to do that conveniently and consistently. You are going to be tasked with understanding your expectations and how they have affected your marriage. Second, you will be asked to evaluate yourself and your marriage. Third, you'll be challenged to make improvements, however small or large, with each list.

Expectations

We all bring expectations into marriage and develop expectations during the marriage. Our personalities, upbringing, experiences, and influences all shape those expectations. I expected marriage to be easy, and Mark expected me to be like him. Our expectations of each other and marriage were unrealistic. In order for our marriage to survive we had to change our expectations.

And that is one of the goals in this book—to change the expectations that need to be changed. To do that we will have to answer some important questions. The big question is: *What do I expect?* Other questions include: *Are my expectations realistic? Are they fair? What should I expect of myself in marriage? What should I expect of my husband?*　　＇

Evaluation

In his book *Leadership Is an Art,* former CEO Max De Pree says that "the first responsibility of a leader is to define reality." We need to stop and measure ourselves. We need to take the time to assess the track we are on before it becomes a runaway train. *How are we doing as a couple, relationally?* That's one question you need to answer, but you also need to have a clear understanding of how your husband feels about your relationship. Does he feel connected, supported, and loved?

Most of the time, couples measure themselves against a very subjective standard: other people and other couples. It's called comparison. The problem with doing so is that others are always an unknown target. We never know what's really going on behind the closed curtains of their lives, and we don't know whether they are even pursuing a true standard. Thus, couples need an objective standard to measure against. One that is always true. God is truth and His revealed, God-breathed Word is completely true. In our lists to love by we always strive to communicate God's precepts and principles for marriage. When people evaluate against God's standards, either their existing expectations will be reinforced or negated, or a new expectation will be created.

Improvements

Once you know what you should expect and have evaluated how you both see your marriage, you can pursue the answer to the question: *How can we do this better?* Couples crave love. If you are reading this book you most likely want to love and be loved. You want a more intimate and fulfilling marriage. The best place to start is by asking: *How can I do this better? What should I do? What should I say?*

WAYS TO USE THIS BOOK

The book is structured with thirty lists for you to learn to love by. At the end of each list, there is a section called "Taking the Next Step." This is your opportunity to work toward building the marriage you want. This may include answering questions, self-evaluation, or taking simple steps to make changes. There are several ways you can use this book to improve your marriage.

Go day by day and repeat. Consistency over time equals impact. The best way to form habits to love well is by committing each day to the thoughts, attitudes, and activities at hand. The lists in this book are easy to read and comprehend. Focus on one each day. Study it, take some time to meditate on it, and apply what you have learned. Don't be overwhelmed. Take small bites. When you have completed the book the first time, start over and go another thirty days. It will reinforce everything you have learned, and you can choose a different task to focus on from the month before. For example, if it is the seventh day of the month, you can focus on one thing from List 7 that your husband would like most. You can then make notes on your husband's reaction and on your progress. If a month later you have mastered that item, you can choose another task from List 7 to work on for the next month.

Some of the action points are not easy to live out, and change does not happen overnight. But little by little, absorbing the truths laid out in this book will bring you closer and closer to the marriage you want.

Skip around. You may have specific challenges in your marriage that you know need work. Before skipping right to those things, we recommend that you begin with List 1. This will lay groundwork that the rest of the book will reinforce. Then go to the specific lists in the table of contents in need of attention in your marriage. You may want to camp out on a certain subject for a significant amount of time before moving on. Some of the concepts in this book, while simple to understand, represent a profound foundational shift that may require an investment of time and energy. Take as much time as you need.

Discuss it with your husband. Involve your husband in what you are processing. There is a counterpart to this book for him called *Lists to Love By for Busy Husbands*. It contains content that is unique to husbands, but it also includes some of the same principles and exercises as this book.

Each list will have questions and subjects to discuss with him. The whole purpose of this book is for you to learn how to love him and connect on a deeper level. His perspective and input is richly essential. Listen to it and value it. Treat his opinion like holy ground. The purpose of this book is not to change your husband, but to change yourself and increase your active love of him.

LISTS TO LOVE BY
FOR BUSY WIVES

LIST 1

7 Truths About Marriage

Imagine you are in your car at a stoplight with another car in the lane to your right. Out of the corner of your eye you start to see the other car steadily inching forward. You wonder to yourself, "Are they moving forward or am I moving backward?" Has that ever happened to you? If so, what is the first thing you do? Well, first, you probably push harder on the brake. But the second thing you do is look for some stationary object that will tell you if you are moving.

A marriage experiences a lot of movements. People change, circumstances change, and culture changes. It's important to have absolute truths about marriage that act as stationary objects that you and your husband can cling to in the midst of a constantly changing world. There are seven truths that we have come to know that keep us grounded.

They become particularly important when we experience rough patches in our relationship.

Truth 1. Marriage is not a quick sprint; it's a lifelong marathon.

A marathon is a long-distance race covering over twenty-six miles. Anyone who has run one will tell you it takes intense training, commitment, discipline, growth, endurance, and resolve. Marriage is the same way. There are attitudes and personality traits that will need training. There are relational muscles that need strengthening. And, most important, it is essential that both a husband and wife enter the marital race to go the distance and finish well.

Truth 2. Marriage is not a fifty-fifty partnership; it's a 100%-100%, give-it-all-you've-got relationship.

All too often, we've heard others say, "Marriage is a fifty-fifty partnership." But that's not true. When we excuse ourselves from putting one hundred percent into the relationship, we will constantly be comparing our efforts against our spouse's and questioning who does more in the relationship. In such a scenario, husbands and wives may even find themselves keeping a marital scorecard of who spends more, disciplines more, does the dishes more, cleans more or works more. Marriage is a 100%-100%, give-it-all-you've-got relationship. Marriage takes total commitment. You can't hold anything back. Day in and day out you have to leave it all on the field.

Truth 3. Marriage is not always a stroll in the park; it's hard work.

Marriage is not easy. A good marriage requires hard work and "heart work." Like most other things in life, when we really work on our marriage, it only gets better and better. And when we really invest our time and energy into our relationship, more often than not, heart transformation occurs as well, which then brings a man and a woman into a more intimate union.

Truth 4. Marriage is not just about two people; it's about two people becoming one flesh.

Our deepest desire in marriage is to know and be known, physically, emotionally, and spiritually. Marriage is about a man and a woman connecting and sharing on all these levels; two separate lives that come together and form one life together. A man and a woman unite and set one direction and vision for their life. They share in each other's pains and triumphs. They share one another's bodies fully

Authors apply to Hefio ♡ ONLY.

with each other. In no other relationship does God call for this type of physical union other than in a husband-and-wife relationship.

Truth 5. Marriage is not just "for better," it's also "for worse."

The most obvious moment of awe in a wedding is when the bride enters, and everyone stands and looks at her. She is glowing. She is striking. Her smile lights up the sanctuary. Awe is also in the face of the groom, who admires and desires her like no other can. The couple then recites their vows, which often include a promise to love one another "for better or worse." But on that day, few brides and grooms are thinking about the "worse" part...they can't imagine there ever being any speed bumps in life or in the relationship. The true character and depth of your committed love for your husband will not be shown in the best of times, but in the worst. Getting through difficult times while staying dedicated to each other shows the power of commitment.

Truth 6. Marriage is not just about happiness; it's about holiness.

Marriage is a holy union between God, a husband, and a wife—a union established to glorify God. God uses marriage to mold and shape us more into His likeness. He exposes our selfishness, refines our attitudes, and builds our character so we may be a better reflection of God. As author John Piper says, "Marriage exists to magnify the truth and worth and beauty and greatness of God."

Truth 7. Marriage is not about getting from your husband; it's about giving to your husband.

Focusing on ourselves will only produce misery. We are called by God to love and sacrifice for our husbands. Marriage is about giving over getting.

TAKING THE NEXT STEP

- On a scale of 1 to 5, where would you rate yourself in your marriage with regard to each truth, with 1 being "Tired and Despairing" and 5 being "Energized and Hopeful"?

- Truth 1. Running the Marathon: Marriage is a long-distance race that requires intense training, commitment, discipline, growth, endurance, and resolve.

  1   2   3   4   5

- Truth 2. Giving 100%: Marriage is a 100%-100%, give-it-all-you've-got relationship. Marriage takes total commitment.

  1   2   3   4   5

- Truth 3. Working Hard: A good marriage requires hard work and "heart work."

  1   2   3   4   5

- Truth 4. Becoming One: Two separate lives come together and form one life physically and spiritually.

  1   2   3   4   5

- Truth 5. For Worse: Marriage is not just "for better," it's also "for worse."

  1   2   3   4   5

- Truth 6. Holiness: God uses marriage to mold and shape us more into His likeness.

  1   2   3   4   5

- Truth 7. Giving over Getting: Marriage is not about getting from your husband; it's about giving to your husband.

  1   2   3   4   5

- Where in your marriage are you tired and where are you energized?

  _____

  _____

- Which truth is most important to you in your marriage right now?

  _____

  _____

- Ask your husband: Which of these truths is most important to you right now? Why?

  _____

  _____

LIST 2

3 Things to Remember About Marriage

When I was seventeen, before I even met Mark, I learned a crucial lesson about what was truly important in life.

I was cheering at my high school football game. It came down to the wire, and as our team pressed hard for a district win we all went crazy with excitement. My heart was racing as I jumped around cheering. Two hours later my heart was still racing, and I was in the hospital emergency room. Alarm emanated from the faces that came in and out of the room as they frantically inserted lines, attached wires, and instructed me on how to trigger my cardiac rhythm to normalcy. The only person who seemed still was the doctor, who was steadily watching a monitor and talking to me. The only thing that was bothering me was the aching arteries in my neck.

Then things changed. My neck started to feel better and my body relaxed. I told the doctor, "I think I'm feeling better." Without taking his eyes off of the monitor he patted my arm and said, "Yes. Yes, you feel better." Several seconds later his demeanor changed and he said to the nurse sharply, "Code Blue." I had a cardiac arrest. As a crowd of hospital workers rushed in around me, all I thought was, "This is serious." Then I felt myself fading away; my thoughts changed. All I could think about was the people I loved. I wondered if they knew how much I loved them. Had I loved them well enough for them to have no doubt?

I was eventually brought back, but my pacemaker and the scars from multiple surgeries are a reminder that my days, and all of our days, are numbered. When we are on our deathbeds, we won't be thinking about all of the things we accomplished or our to-do lists. We will remember the people we love most.

If we are to make a marriage last a lifetime, until that day when death do us part, we need to make every day count by loving our husbands well. Here are three things to remember to help you do that.

1. Remember your vow of love.

"To have and to hold, from this day forward, for better, for worse, for richer, for poorer, in sickness and in health, to love and to cherish 'til death do us part." The day you and your husband were married was the day you promised all these things as you stood before God, before your family, and before your friends. Remember, this commitment you made was meant to be lifelong, and calling it quits would break that unconditional promise you once made with all your heart.

2. Remember your vow of commitment.

At the time of our marriage Mark couldn't have imagined what the commitment to love me in sickness and in health would entail. During the course of our marriage, I have had a ton of health issues due to my heart. He had no idea that there would be an entire year where I was unable to get out of bed because of my condition. But he made a commitment to me, for better or worse. Things can always get worse. Marriage was never meant to be a contract to be broken, but a covenant to be cherished. In his care for me, Mark demonstrated his commitment to me. It wasn't based on what I could do for him as in a contract. His commitment was a sacrificial action. Below is an outline of the difference between signing a contract and entering into a covenant.

Covenant	Contract
Based on unconditional love between God, a husband, and a wife	Based on conditional consideration between two people
Sacrificial Action (i.e., I'll do it no matter what you do)	Reciprocal Transaction (e.g., If you do this, then and only then will I do that)
Based on Mutual Commitment	Based on Mutual Distrust
Seeks to Give	Seeks to Get
For Life	For Now

In a nutshell, a contract is all about what you get. A covenant is all about what you give. Marriage is a covenant.

3. Remember the purpose of marriage.

As I said at the beginning of the book, I thought when I got married I would simply live happily ever after. Did you ever think that? It doesn't take much experience in marriage to discover that this simply isn't true. The only person who can ever provide ultimate joy for you is God, *not* your husband. Perhaps realizing this truth means changing your expectations of him. Remember from the seven truths in List 1, marriage is not ultimately about happiness, but about holiness. It's a holy union between God, a husband, and a wife—a union established to glorify God. It's a way for Him to refine us.

TAKING THE NEXT STEP

- What was your favorite memory from your wedding day? Why?

  _____

  _____

- Ask your husband the same question.

  _____

  _____

- Based on how well you have lovingly followed through on your vows, grade yourself (A through F). Then have your husband grade himself.

You	*Your Husband*
____For better, for worse.	____For better, for worse.
____For richer, for poorer.	____For richer, for poorer.
____In sickness and in health.	____In sickness and in health.
____To love and to cherish.	____To love and to cherish.
____'Til death do you part.	____'Til death do you part

- What vow will you commit to work on starting today?

  _____

  _____

LIST 3

5 Powerful Words for Your Marriage

This is something that we have gone back and forth about for our entire twenty-seven-year marriage. Words. Words are very important to Mark. He was an attorney, so he enjoys analyzing the meaning and significance of words. My problem is that I normally shoot from the hip and don't always think through the things I say before saying them. We have had many long conversations about something I have said.

Words do have tremendous power. There are several types of words that will soften your husband's heart. However, it is equally important to have the right tone to accompany those words. Respectful words are the most important for Mark, as they are with most husbands. Whenever Mark would be critical of me I would get bitter, and while I may have used respectful words, I would say them with an insincere tone. It wasn't just enough to use the right types of words. They had to be said with sincerity. With that said, here are five types of powerful words to use with your husband that will draw you closer together.

1. Respectful words.

Like I said, this one is most important to Mark. After years of being married, it's easy to become comfortable with one another. But sometimes that comfort can turn into a lack of respect when you are no longer careful with what comes out of your mouth. Choosing to speak respectfully to your husband, and about your husband, means choosing words that will honor him, not undermine him. It also means choosing words that affirm his judgment and abilities, like "I really respect the decision you made."

2. Affirming words.

We can tell you from experience that our need for affirmation doesn't disappear with age. We both still desire to be validated by one another—and we desire that validation often. Cherish your husband by saying things like "You did a great job coaching our child on how to handle that issue" or "I was so impressed by the leadership you showed at work today."

3. Caring words.

It's easy to choose to dismiss your husband's need for attention. There are so many things to focus on, particularly kids, if you have them, or the never-ending household to-do list. But we encourage you to sit down and give your full attention to your husband when he needs you. Speak caring words to him in a moment when he needs to know someone is on his side. "I'm so sorry to hear that…" or "Tell me more about how you are feeling" are caring words that will give life into your relationship.

4. Encouraging words.

Truett Cathy, the founder of Chick-fil-A, once said to Mark, "How do you know if someone needs encouragement? If they are breathing!" Everyone needs to hear words of encouragement, especially our husbands. They mean the most when they come from his wife. And that can mean the difference between pressing on or giving up when someone is discouraged. Encourage your husband to press on.

5. Appreciative words.

Finally, it's important to speak words of appreciation to your husband. No one wants to feel taken for granted. Keep your eyes open for ways to express appreciation to him. "Thank you for how hard you work" or "I'm so grateful for your help on that project" are the types of words that will uplift him and show your appreciation to him.

TAKING THE NEXT STEP

- List in order the two types of words that are most important to your husband. Then ask him which ones are most important to him and compare your answers.

You	*Your Husband*
1. _____	**1.** _____
2. _____	**2.** _____

- What is one type that you need to focus more on? Concentrate today on using the types of words you need to focus on. For example, if it is appreciative words, then write down one or two appreciative things you can say to your husband and say them. Take note of your husband's response.

_____

_____

_____

_____

LIST 4

∿

5 Things Wives Should Stop Doing

Oftentimes it is the small things that we do or say that mean the most to our husbands. Mark and I were getting ready to go out on a date and our kids were young. It has always been difficult for me to leave our children. One of my daughters was clinging to my leg, crying and begging me to stay. I got down on my knees and looked her straight in the eye and told her that my relationship with her dad was really important and that I needed to be with him, just the two of us, at that moment. I'll never forget how much that meant to Mark. He still talks about it years later.

I wasn't always good at putting Mark first. Many times I would think, "My husband is fine. After all, we are a team in what we do." I thought of him as an extension of myself, two more hands to keep our family of seven operable. I didn't consider that he needed me. Too often I put my energy toward everything and everyone else. I tended to throw myself into any activity my kids were involved in. I would be the team mom for football, chorus, you name it. It took a long time, but I finally realized that I needed to stop and make Mark my top priority. Our marriage got a lot better after that—learn from me!

Here are five things I've learned over the years that all wives should stop doing.

1. Don't put anything before your husband.

I thought I could do it all and meet everyone else's needs. I couldn't. If you don't make your husband a top priority, your marriage will suffer. Remember to give your husband your freshest and best, not your leftovers.

2. Don't expect your husband to be your girlfriend.

He converses differently. He thinks differently. He processes things differently. So don't treat him like your girlfriends or be frustrated if he doesn't respond to you as a girlfriend would.

3. Don't dishonor your husband.

You can dishonor your spouse by the way you talk about him in a negative light to others; by the way you talk to him as if he were a child (I am superguilty of this one) or an idiot; or simply with your tone of voice. Be careful not to question his judgment and abilities. That doesn't mean you can't offer your opinion. Just make sure he knows that you trust him and his judgment even when you disagree.

4. Don't use sex to bargain with your husband.

Your sexual relationship is not a game. It should not be used to get what you want. It should not be withheld as a form of punishment to make him change his mind and give you what you want. Sex should be a very important part of your relationship. It is not something that must be earned by your husband, but rather should be freely given in your marriage relationship.

5. Don't expect your husband to be Prince Charming.

News flash...no husband is the perfect Prince Charming of your dreams. If you keep expecting him to meet every dreamy expectation you have, you're bound to be disappointed and he's bound to feel wholly inadequate. Try to focus on the things about him that are charming, the qualities you saw in him when you fell in love.

TAKING THE NEXT STEP

* Go back and star the top thing you need to stop doing. Then commit to stop. To ensure that the habit is broken, you may want to ask someone to hold you accountable.

  _____

  _____

* The things you need to stop doing may be deeply rooted habits. Habits can be hard to break, but if you keep repeating the thirty lists in this book it will reinforce the changes you are making, and you can add things to work on.

LIST 5

3 Keys to Unlock the Door to Intimacy

Trust is an essential ingredient in the two of you becoming one. Perhaps you've had a breach of trust in your relationship. When trust is broken, it creates a chasm that you feel can never be filled. Don't look down into the chasm, look up. Looking down into it will make it seem too deep. Looking up will focus your attention on a big God who will build the bridge to trust one step at a time. We don't want to minimize the deep hurt and wound that a violation of trust causes. That is real and valid. But we encourage you to take the thoughts below to your husband and let him know you are willing to start the process of building back the trust.

If trust needs to be restored from a wrongdoing, the wrong needs to be admitted, and the admission should be accompanied by a sincere request for forgiveness followed by the granting of forgiveness by the offended mate. We'll talk more about forgiveness in List 13.

You may be thinking you haven't done anything wrong. That's the wrong way to think. We all make mistakes in our words, in our thoughts, in our actions.

Whether building trust or restoring it, trust is not something that someone owes you. Trust must be earned. That means that you need to provide something to your husband in order for him to trust you. It is not something you do just one time but consistently, day in and day out, over a period of time.

If trust is the door to intimacy, then there are three keys to opening that door. In order to trust you, your husband must have complete confidence in the following from this day forward.

1. You are who you say you are.

Your husband needs to know that everything about you is real. Whether you are with your family, friends, or coworkers, your husband needs to see that you are the same person wherever you are and whoever you are with. He needs to see you living a consistent life. Your husband needs to know that you are rock solid, not a person whose personality or behavior is constantly shifting. Consistency is the key!

Also, when you and your husband got married, you promised to be there for each other "for better, for worse, for richer, for poorer, in sickness and in health…'til death do us part." You also committed to become "one flesh." That means the other person should be able to rely upon those promises—that you will not tear the marriage apart and that you will be there, as his wife, no matter what happens.

2. You will always speak the truth.

There are no such things as "little white lies" or "half truths." What you say is either true or it is not. Let me illustrate. If your husband asks you something simple, like "What have you been doing?" don't just say, "Doing the laundry." If you have also been watching television and checking Facebook, say so. Remember: Truth is the whole truth. To build trust, speak truth in everything, big and small. Doing so will help build your husband's confidence in your trustworthiness.

Speaking truth also means not keeping secrets from him. Whether it's a purchase you made, an addiction you have, an illness you're experiencing, or a place you've been, nothing should be kept from your husband. Keeping fun surprises may be an exception, but there is a significant difference between surprises and secrets.

3. You will always do what you say you'll do.

In simple terms, when you say you'll do something, the other person can *check it off the list* or *take it to the bank*. It's a *done deal*. If for some reason you are unable to do it, let the other person know immediately. Also, the seeds of suspicion and distrust seem to germinate when the person working to rebuild the trust does unpredictable things. For example, if you are going to be unusually late for any reason, tell your husband and let him know why.

As you rebuild trust in your relationship, remember that one of the best things you can do is to ask your husband, "What can I do to earn your trust again?" Then be sure to listen carefully and take action.

TAKING THE NEXT STEP

- In what ways are you different around friends and coworkers than you are around your family?

  _____

  _____

- Is there anywhere in your life where you speak so-called half truths or embellish?

  _____

  _____

- Make a list of the promises you made this week. Did you follow through? If not, why?

                              Promise

1. _____ Kept? _____ Yes _____ No

   Why?_____

2. _____ Kept? _____ Yes _____ No

   Why?_____

3. _____ Kept? _____ Yes _____ No

   Why?_____

LIST 6

~

5 Unfair Expectations You May Have of Your Husband

"You and Mark are like two ships passing in the night." Those were the words of our premarital counselor. We had both taken personality tests and the results showed how different we were. I'll admit that when he said those words I really didn't see it. We had a great time dating, and I felt we were so similar in our approach to life and worldviews. The big difference between Mark and me lies in the way we think. Mark thinks concretely, focusing on the facts, while I think abstractly, pulling in perceptions beyond what is apparent. It is easier for me to read between the lines of situations, and so I usually understand how Mark feels about things at all times. I get him. I assumed Mark could read me, too. I had the expectation that he got me.

He didn't. There were so many situations where my feelings were hurt because I had an expectation that was unfair. Things that bother me don't necessarily bother him, so he has trouble empathizing. He tries hard to understand me as best as he can. Over the years he has learned the right things to say, but it is difficult for him to fully comprehend what I am feeling. I am okay with that now, but I wasn't back then. My expectation early in our marriage was unfair.

Problems in marriage often start with unfair and unreal expectations that husbands and wives have of one another. Unreal expectations become unmet expectations, which become unsettling issues in a marriage. So here are five expectations that may be hurting your husband and your marriage.

1. Expect that he should get you.

As you see from our experience, the differences between men and women—how we think and act—are obvious and even humorous at times. But when a wife expects that her husband should completely understand her, see things through her lens and from her perspective, it creates unreal expectations that are impossible for him to fulfill.

2. Expect that he will never be tempted by other women.

Men are wired visually. All men are tempted. It's a fact that makes life difficult for every guy living in this sex-obsessed culture. When a wife expects that he will never be tempted, she is ignoring this fact. On the other hand, it is fair for her to expect that he will resist that temptation. It's important for a wife to understand this reality and for her to support her husband in the fight against temptation.

3. Expect that he will always make you happy.

This expectation often starts in the early years of marriage, when you think you and your handsome prince will live happily ever after because he will always make you happy. But then, the passage of time reveals the gritty truth that a husband will disappoint his wife at some point. So if you rely completely on your husband to bring you ultimate happiness, marriage problems are bound to occur.

4. Expect that he can read your mind.

This expectation often occurs during arguments when you don't really want to, or don't feel you should have to, explain what you're thinking. Hints and subtle comments do not help your husband as much as a straightforward explanation. The more you are willing to share what you're really thinking, the more he will be able to anticipate and understand what you're thinking down the road. But he'll never be able to get it right every time.

5. Expect that he will have the same daily priorities as you do.

Many Saturday mornings we have started the day thinking we were on the same page, only to discover that the plans we had were different. I'll be thinking about a project list that we need to be working on, while Mark is thinking about spending the morning relaxing together. However that may play out for you, it's a sure thing that when you expect your husband to wake up with your priorities on his mind, you may not be pleased with the result.

So be sure that your expectations of your husband are realistic. And keep communicating and forgiving him if he can't read your mind along the way!

TAKING THE NEXT STEP

- What are some of the unreal expectations you've put on your husband? Can't think of any? Ask him.

  _____

  _____

- The night before your next day off together, ask him, "What would you like to do most tomorrow?" Then make his day and make it happen.

LIST 7

〜

10 Things Husbands Want to Hear from Their Wives

When I was in college I had a roommate that guys always wanted to date. In fact, she would often be dating two or three guys at one time. It was a curious thing to me. Why didn't she choose one? Why didn't they get mad that she didn't choose one? I remember asking her about it. And she answered very honestly that she liked all of them. There were traits about each of them that she admired. And that was why they all wanted to be with her! There was something very attractive about the way she admired, complimented, and looked up to them. She made men feel adored. She wasn't being insincere or playing a game. It was her natural tendency to see the best in people, guys and girls alike, and to point it out. It was a gift that made her a great date or, in my case, a great friend.

I'm not good at that. Making my husband feel like he is the best is something I need to work on. Seeing how he responds to it makes working on it worth it. It's like giving him his favorite meal to eat. There is nothing like specific and detailed praise and validation to energize a man and a marriage. After surveying many husbands, we found these are the ten most common things husbands want to hear from their wives.

1. "I love being your wife."

As simple as it sounds, husbands want to know that their wives are content in their marriage and truly enjoy just being with them. When is the last time you thanked your husband for marrying you? Don't just assume he knows. Tell him!

2. "You're an outstanding father."

Deep down every man has the desire to be seen as a hero—especially to his children. Specifically, tell your husband why he is your kids' hero. And tonight, at dinner, tell your children why he is so special.

3. "I'm really attracted to you. You are the man!"

It's a myth that women are always more looks conscious than men. As guys' hairlines begin to recede and stomachs start protruding, they can become quite sensitive about their appearance. Never joke about how your husband looks. Tell him he's hot and how attracted you are to him.

4. "I support the decision you made."

When a man makes a decision, especially a tough one, he doesn't want his wife being critical of it or questioning him about it. He wants to know that his wife is behind him and admires his ability to make good decisions.

5. "I know how important it is to live within our means. I'm with you on this."

Your husband is concerned about the future of your family. So that means he is concerned about taking care of his family financially. Having a wife he can rely on to spend and save wisely is a tremendous comfort to him.

6. "I'm so grateful for your spiritual leadership."

All of us are hardwired for a relationship with God, and many men want to be seen as the spiritual leaders of their families. Encourage your husband in his faith and for taking his role as a spiritual leader seriously.

7. "You are so wise."

Many men are born problem solvers and relish the process of thinking through something and arriving at a solution. This, incidentally, is why your husband is always trying to fix your problems when all you want him to do is listen. Recognizing your husband's mental prowess and complimenting him on his intelligence will pay massive dividends to you. Emphasize to him that you trust his wise judgment.

8. "I appreciate how hard you work to provide for our family."

There are many things in life that your husband cannot control, but one he can control is effort. It brings him great pleasure to work hard and see the results. To directly control and be the man responsible for creating something from nothing thrills him. Encourage his great work ethic.

9. "Thank you very much for helping me with that."

When a man serves his wife, he wants her to recognize it. A simple thank-you is all he needs.

10. "I'm impressed with how you handled that situation."

Sometimes a wife will point out when her husband does not handle something well. So when he handles a particularly difficult situation well, let him know.

TAKING THE NEXT STEP

- Star the list items you usually say. Circle the items you don't say. Ask your husband which are the most important to him, and focus on those.

  _____

  _____

- What are other things your husband wants to hear from you? Add to the list here.

  _____

  _____

LIST 8

5 Things Husbands Wish Wives Knew

On one particular Saturday I was spending time with some friends. Little did I know that Mark was at home working on all the laundry as a surprise for me. We have five kids, so laundry is not an easy task. For four hours he worked, sorting, washing, drying, and folding. When I got home I walked into the house, and he was standing there waiting for me with an anticipatory smile. Then he pointed to the stacks of freshly folded laundry. My distracted response was "Oh, you did the laundry. Thank you." Then I went upstairs to change. It was like I popped a balloon—with just seven words I totally deflated my husband.

When Mark does something around the house he gives a report because he likes validation. "I fixed the locks on the door!" "I just cleaned out the pool." It's important to him that the value of his work is appreciated. My daughters are great at it. When he does something for them they'll say, "Dad, you're the best." It makes him feel great when they do it, but most of the time he's looking to hear it from me. It took me a while to learn that.

There are many things that husbands wish their wives knew. Most of them are simple things we can do or say in just a few minutes. In my case, it would have taken only two minutes to really praise Mark for four hours of work. Knowing what your husband desires is the key to investing your time wisely and getting the greatest return for your marriage. Here are five things your husband may wish you knew about what he desires.

1. He desires validation.

Your husband wants to hear "You are the man!" from you. When he does something well, he wants you to take notice and affirm him. No one is able to validate a husband like his wife.

2. He desires respect.

We talked about this one before. Your husband wants you to respect his judgment. A man needs his woman to value and trust his opinions and decisions, even if they prove to be wrong sometimes. That means not constantly questioning his knowledge with a "Why do you say that?" or challenging his decisions by asking, "Why don't you just stop and get directions?" He also wants you to respect his abilities. A man doesn't want to hear something like "You're not a handyman, I'll call the plumber" or "Sports aren't your thing. I'll ask John to teach him how to throw the football." A guy doesn't want to be shot down before he even gives it a chance.

3. He desires conciseness.

Men simply want the bottom line. Many times I'll give all the background, tell all the stories, and give numerous details. That's fine, but sometimes it's hard for Mark to sift through all of that. It's easier for him if I am just clear and concise with what I want him to do, and eliminate unnecessary details.

4. He desires forgiveness.

All husbands mess up. Most of the time it is not intentional. When he asks for forgiveness, you need to grant it to him, not hold a grudge against him and continue to bring up his historical mistakes. There is freedom in forgiveness. We don't want to suggest that this is easy, and there are definitely violations of trust that may take time to forgive. We'll go into more detail about forgiveness in List 13.

5. He desires support.

Husbands and wives were designed to complement each other, not compete with each other. He needs to know that you are on his team, that you really want to help and support him, that you've got his back all the time. When he has to make a tough decision, when he loses a job, when he's struggling—he needs to know you are with him all the way.

TAKING THE NEXT STEP

- What does your husband desire most—validation, respect, conciseness, forgiveness, or support?

  _____

  _____

- How do you plan to meet that need today?

  _____

  _____

LIST 9

⤳

11 Things a Husband and Wife Must Agree On

In 1776, after the Declaration of Independence was signed, the American colonies took a huge step into the unknown. There was agreement that they no longer wanted to be identified with Great Britain, but they had no clear understanding of how to form the nation they wanted to become. The members of the Continental Congress agreed that there should be a central government, but they did not want that government to have a ruling power or king. The Articles of Confederation were drafted as an attempt to bring unity to the country, but its limited federal authority created many problems. Unless something was changed, the lack of central strength threatened the nation's existence.

In 1787, a Constitutional Convention was held to "create a more perfect union." After heated debate, a carefully crafted Constitution and Bill of Rights was agreed upon. While it wasn't perfect, it is still the structure the delegates sculpted to govern the United States.

When a couple gets engaged to be married they are heading into the unknown. They agree on the importance of unity and want to pursue a more perfect union. But they don't know what their marriage is going to look like. There's bound to be disagreement. However, forming a more perfect union in marriage requires coming to agreement on certain foundational principles. It is their constitution, so to speak. It may take some debating, but building the foundation is paramount to the strength of your marriage. This list is the foundation that has governed us.

1. **You are married for life. Therefore, divorce should never be considered, except possibly for unfaithfulness, abuse, or abandonment; and even then only after seeking wise counsel and applying God's word to your situation.**

2. **Your marriage is a top priority, and you will do whatever you need to do to strengthen it.**

3. **You will strive to meet the sexual needs of your mate. Sex will not be withheld as punishment or because of lack of interest.**

4. You will always be honest with your spouse and will speak the truth in love. That means no secrets.

5. You must agree on whether or not you would like to have children.

6. You must agree on when and how you will discipline your children.

7. You must agree under what moral code or belief system you will raise your kids.

8. You and your husband will always honor your parents, but you and your husband—not your parents or in-laws—will make the decisions in your marriage and for your children.

9. You must agree on how much you will spend, save, and share.

10. You must agree on where you will worship.

11. You must agree on your career priorities. Whose career will become the focus: Will he work? Will you work? Will you work inside or outside your home?

TAKING THE NEXT STEP

- What items above are foundational for your marriage? Make a list. What would you add to the list above?

  _____

  _____

- Share your list with your husband and ask him what would be important to him.

  _____

  _____

- If you disagree on a point, what can you do to fully understand your husband and see things from his perspective?

  _____

  _____

LIST 10

◦───◦

8 Keys to Understanding What Your Husband Is Really Saying

Mark and I have opposite communication styles. Completely opposite. And we work together. Forty hours a week. The opportunities for misunderstanding are endless! There have been times when we will be in a meeting with ten people, and he and I will be the only two people who don't understand each other. It can be exasperating.

We all edit our words. We take what we are thinking in our heads and say it, but shorten it to get it out faster. Sometimes we lose the meaning in the process. Husbands are no different. Do you ever feel like you are not getting the full picture of what he really means below the surface?

Girls, in my effort to help you better understand and communicate with your husband, I'm going to share with you a sample of the Mark Merrill male code. This code has taken me two decades to decipher, because it really has no rhyme or reason. It is my hope it will be a jumping-off point for you to understand your own husband's code. Unless, of course, he speaks English.

1. "Is something wrong?" means *It's obvious something's wrong, so please don't make me guess.*

Your husband can't read minds. He is saying, *I know you are upset, but I have no idea why.* He really doesn't know. So even though you want him to always understand why you're upset, this simply isn't possible. Instead of making him guess, it's important to recognize this question as your husband's desire to know what's bothering you without getting annoyed that he doesn't know already.

2. "Can we talk about this later?" means *I need a break from thinking and I really don't want to deal with this right now. Or I can only focus on one thing at a time, and I need to focus on what I'm doing right now.*

You have something you want to talk about, and to you it is urgent. When you hear your husband say this, you assume he must not see the issue as important enough to discuss right now. But the truth is, there are certain distractions keeping him from giving his best in that moment. It usually means he's tired, hungry, or preoccupied. So rather than push to talk about it this instant, give your husband time to get in the right frame of mind to process it.

3. "I hear you" means *You've said that a number of times and you don't need to say it again.*

When your husband tells you that he hears you, it means that he wants you to stop repeating it because he's got it. Continuing to say the same thing over and over again is overkill. He heard you, he's got it, and he wants to move on. I tend to repeat myself if I don't get the reaction I need from Mark, instead of stopping and explaining that his reaction does not match the importance of what I am telling him. This usually happens when I am explaining an incident with our children.

4. "I've got this" means *Don't instruct me on how to do it.*

Your husband likes to be in charge and figure things out on his own. So when he says he can handle it, the last thing he wants is for you to step in and tell him what to do. He wants you to trust him to do things the right way, to believe in him, and to support him. So give your husband the freedom to fail or succeed on his own when it comes to things like figuring out directions, fixing something around the house, or handling a situation with your child. This often is a carryover habit from instructing children all day. I instruct Mark, too.

5. "Sure, that's fine" means *I really don't have a strong opinion about it.*

A classic example of this is when an engaged couple is making decisions about their wedding. When the man doesn't give much input about what sort of flowers or centerpieces would be best, the woman might assume he must not care. But you must come to understand (sometimes) your man really doesn't feel strongly about certain things one way or another. He trusts your ability to make the call, and there is freedom in that!

6. "How are you feeling?" means *I'm trying to show you that I care about you.*

I think most of us would agree that women's emotions are more complicated than those of men. So this question demonstrates your husband's effort to get on the same page as you. He senses something is not right, but he doesn't know how to read your emotions and he needs you to tell him. It's important for you not to mistake this question from your husband as just health related. Rather, this is a heart-related question that a man asks in order to show he cares.

7. "I just did the dinner dishes. What else can I do to help?" means *I'm trying to help you with things around the house now so that I can be physically intimate with you later.*

This is actually something that I decoded about Mark a long time ago. It became obvious that his real motive was not just to help me. When he does the dishes, he'll jokingly say something like "Hey honey, I'm doing the dishes now!" Then he winks. It makes me laugh. His rationale is: if I do the dishes while she settles the kids then she won't be so tired and can go to bed earlier! Though, to his credit, he does plenty of vacuuming, laundry, and other things around the house—without any expectation of intimacy in return.

8. "I just fixed the leaking faucet" means *I'm trying to impress you with my handyman skills, and I want you to notice.*

He wants to be your hero. Men like to build things, make things, repair things, and fix things to impress their wives. As I've shared before, when Mark fixes the broken toilet, he really likes it when I say something like "Wow. You did that? You are the man!"

While there is so much more to decode, I hope this helps you to better understand your husband.

TAKING THE NEXT STEP

- What do you think your husband says often while actually meaning something else? Are any of them on this list?

  _____

  _____

- Think about the ways that you communicate. Are you straightforward and clear? In other words, are there things that you say that your husband needs to decode?

  _____

  _____

- If you were graded on listening and understanding your husband, what grade would you get?

  _____

  _____

LIST 11

~~~

5 Ways to Harden Your Heart

She went on Facebook because she was a little lonely and bored. It was a fun way to pass the time and distract herself from the daily stress. When she friended a guy from high school there was nothing to be ashamed of, because it was out of nostalgia and curiosity, not attraction. Here and there they would like or comment on one another's statuses and pictures. It grew, and soon they were sending each other private messages.

As she got to know him she started to focus on the things they had in common. The more she focused on it, the more convinced she became that she had more in common with this man than her own husband. She even started to question whether or not she ever loved her husband. This unfortunate true story doesn't end well. She ended up leaving her husband to be with the other man, only to leave that man shortly after that.

Becoming hard-hearted toward a spouse is a slow road of poor decisions and disengagement. Love is a day-by-day, hour-by-hour, even minute-by-minute choice. There are decisions you can make to grow your love and decisions you can make to elicit the opposite outcome. If you want to love your husband well, then avoid doing these five things, which will harden your heart toward your husband.

1. Be critical of him.

You don't even have to be vocal about it. If you focus your time thinking about all the negative qualities of your husband, he will be defined that way in your mind. His identity to you will become an embodiment of short-comings. Take time to think about, and perhaps write down, the things about your husband that you are grateful for.

2. Go comparison shopping.

This is what happened to the couple in the story. Usually it starts out small, but then it grows into something massive. A slight irritation with a certain characteristic of your husband and an admiration of a quality in another man starts to occupy your mind. It's playing with fire. And we all know what happens when you play with fire. You get burned. The woman in the story found that out the hard way.

3. Focus on your needs, your needs, your needs.

Make the marriage center around all your wants and needs. Focus on whether or not your husband fulfills you. When we focus solely on ourselves, we tend to zero in on the things we don't have rather than being grateful for the things we do have. Taking an attitude of selflessness and seeking to meet the needs of others produces the opposite result.

4. Don't have sex.

Having sex is like working out. When it's not being done it seems like work that you have to do. However, when we are in the habit of doing it we may even want to do it more. It adds health and intimacy to the relationship.

5. Have unrealistic standards for your relationship.

Many people get unrealistic standards from movies and television. In those forms of media, relationships have a level of passion that cannot last the long term. It is a half-hour to two-hour sprint, and yet we compare our marriages to an unreachable form of passionate bliss. A real marriage is a partnership for experiencing both the joys and struggles of life. Your husband will never live up to a scripted, studio-dressed, and carefully filmed leading man.

TAKING THE NEXT STEP

- What does your husband do well? Make a list.

  _____

  _____

- Have any of these negative attitudes or actions crept into your marriage? Commit yourself to eliminating it by listing an opposite action that you are going to do this week.

  _____

  _____

6 Reasons Your Married Sex Life Lacks Passion

When you got married, you didn't imagine this was how it would be. After all, you love each other. You are attracted to one another and have good chemistry. However, when you are intimate, there is something missing. Maybe it is a new development in your relationship. Maybe the busyness of life, indifference, or even bitterness have created a chasm in your marriage. Or, perhaps it has always been that way and you hoped it would eventually change, but it hasn't. Your married sex life is passionless.

Sex is not always going to be earth-shattering. But when it consistently lacks passion over time, it can become divisive. The frequency of its occurrence tends to become less and less. Filled with unsatisfied desires, some turn to unhealthy things such as porn or an affair to attempt to quench their thirst. Others just stop initiating altogether. In order to find the solution, it is important to identify the underlying problem. If your married sex life lacks passion, it could be because of one of these reasons.

1. Inhibitions.

When a husband or wife are inhibited, it normally comes from a negative view of sex. This negative view may have formed from something as dramatic as abuse. Others may have had parents who, with very good and honorable intentions, tried to dissuade them from having unmarried sex by communicating that all sex is bad. That association sometimes remains even after marriage. Feelings of guilt, fear, and self-consciousness come rushing in, as if they are still doing something wrong. Unfortunately, these are normally deeply engrained (particularly abuse) and the person may need counseling to move toward healing.

2. Lack of prioritizing and initiative.

Sex is not set as a priority. Energy is given to everything else: raising kids, pursuing careers, or maybe even pursuing other people. This normally happens when one person puts sex low on the list, leaving the other frustrated. Picking up on the frustration of their spouse, they do it out of obligation. Nothing takes the passion out of physical intimacy more than when a husband feels like his wife has sex with him as a favor or vice versa. Both husband and wife need to keep it high on the list of priorities.

3. Hidden bitterness.

When unresolved issues and a lack of forgiveness linger below the surface, they create disunity. Passionate sex is fueled by the level of connection a couple is experiencing. Undealt-with hurt will turn the heart into a petri dish of bitterness. The relationship electricity will falter until it eventually shuts off.

4. Lack of honesty.

Whether it is for fear of either rejection or hurting the other person, a lack of honesty will place limits on the sexual relationship in a marriage. It shows a lack of trust. It's important to be able to communicate what each person finds enjoyable and what they don't. This doesn't mean all desires need to be met, but that there should be a safe environment for free and open dialogue. One of the beautiful things about physical intimacy is knowing things about one another that no one else knows.

5. Loss of attractiveness.

This can be physical, but in most cases it is deeper. Maybe it is the abrasive or disrespectful way she treats him that causes him to view her as less attractive. It could be that he has a lack of initiative in life or with the family, and it turns her off. For example, he may have become a couch potato or be content in a life that lacks any kind of personal growth. On the other hand, the attractiveness of her husband may increase for her if he planned adventures for the family and continually challenged himself personally and professionally. Address the issues honestly but with kindness and gentleness.

6. Familiarity.

Both of you are caught in a cycle of doing the same routine. It's gotten predictable and boring. A couple can easily fall into this trap, but it's important to change things up and perhaps even try something new that you both are comfortable with.

TAKING THE NEXT STEP

- Which of these do you and your husband struggle with?

  _____

  _____

- When you think about these, do any seem to be a risk to your sex life?

  _____

  _____

- What about your husband turns you on? Does he know?

  _____

  _____

- Rate the Passion of Your Sexual Intimacy:

  Touching

  Low 1   2   3   4   5   **High**

  Kissing

  Low 1   2   3   4   5   **High**

  Talking

  Low 1   2   3   4   5   **High**

Frequency

Low 1   2   3   4   5   **High**

Variety

Low 1   2   3   4   5   **High**

Buildup

Low 1   2   3   4   5   **High**

Attractiveness

Low 1   2   3   4   5   **High**

- Have your husband rate the above as well and discuss together.
- Ask your husband: What things do you want me to do more when we are making love? What are things you don't like?

_____

_____

LIST 13

~~

4 Decisions That Define Forgiveness

As the man approached her, she wondered what to do. A flood of emotions poured into her mind, reminding her of the horrid pain this man had brought upon her.

During World War II, Corrie ten Boom and her family saved Jews from being sent off to concentration camps by hiding them in a room at the top of their home. When Nazi officers learned what was going on, the house was raided and Corrie was sent to a prison, a political concentration camp, and finally a death camp. But, miraculously, she survived.

Corrie had to overcome many moments of hardship even after the war ended. This was one of them. She was speaking at a church when she saw a former SS man, a soldier in the organization under Hitler that carried out genocidal killing and many other war crimes. This particular SS man had guarded her in the concentration camp. And he was directly involved with the death of her beloved sister at that camp. Now he was coming over to shake her hand. Even though Corrie often spoke of the need to forgive others, she knew she couldn't forgive this man in her own strength. God had to do it through her. Corrie wrote, "When He tells us to love our enemies, He gives, along with the command, the love itself." God gave Corrie the strength to forgive and love the man when she herself could not.

Perhaps you've never had to deal with such heavy forgiveness in your life as Corrie ten Boom had, but there are many times in life when you will have to both forgive and be forgiven in your marriage. When you are wronged by your husband you have a choice. You can choose to hold on to the hurt and spend the rest of your life with the pain, bitterness, and anger. Or you can choose to be released from it, healed, and freed. It's a decision to forgive the person who has hurt you.

So let's talk about what forgiveness really is. When you really forgive someone, you are making a decision to release, embrace, pardon, and grow.

1. A decision to release.

In the process of forgiving, the first barrier you have to remove is within your own mind. You must make the decision: *I will not dwell on this incident.* Don't replay the incident in your mind. We realize that is easy to say but hard to do. When that reel begins to play in your mind, intentionally push the Stop button. Realize that it will not make things better. Dwell on what is good and ask God to give you the strength to withstand the onslaught of those attacks on your mind. When you forgive, you are also proactively choosing to release your bitterness, resentment, vengeance, and anger toward the person who has hurt you.

2. A decision to embrace.

When you truly forgive, you are intentionally embracing mercy and grace. Putting it simply, mercy is not giving someone what they deserve. Grace is giving someone what they don't deserve. Why show mercy and grace to this person who has deeply hurt you? For two reasons: First, God extends his perfect mercy and grace to you. And He showers His perfect love upon you...every time, all the time. Second, remember the Golden Rule? It basically says, "Treat others as you want to be treated." So when you make a bad mistake, when you hurt someone, when you wrong someone, how do you want to be treated?

3. A decision to pardon.

Merriam-Webster's Learner's Dictionary defines *pardon* as "an act of officially saying that someone who was judged to be guilty of a crime will be allowed to go free and will not be punished." Mark remembers from his days of practicing law that once someone is pardoned or acquitted in a court of law, they cannot be tried again for the same offense. That's called double jeopardy. So when you choose to pardon your offender by forgiving them, you are letting go of your right to punish them for the offense in the future. You are basically saying, *I will not bring this incident up again and use it against you*. In so doing, you are choosing to hold on to the person, not the offense.

In our twenty-seven years of marriage, we have forgiven each other for numerous offenses and hurts in our relationship—or at least we thought we had. There have been occasions where one of us has brought up a past offense the other thought was pardoned, only to find that court was still in session on the issue. Real forgiveness must involve a complete pardon.

4. A decision to grow.

When you forgive, you are taking away the power the wrongdoing wields over you and using that power toward your growth, perhaps the growth of your relationship. You are making the statement: *I will not allow this matter to stand between us or hinder our personal relationship.* Think of forgiveness as something that will change your life—by bringing you peace, emotional and spiritual healing, and hope—and, hopefully, the life of the one you have forgiven.

TAKING THE NEXT STEP

- What is a situation where you needed to be forgiven?

  _____

  _____

- What is the hardest thing you have forgiven your husband for? How did you feel afterward? What were the results?

  _____

  _____

- Is there anyone whom you need to forgive today?

  _____

  _____

- Is there anything for which you need to ask for forgiveness?

  _____

  _____

LIST 14

10 Texts to Send Your Husband in the Next Ten Days

Can you remember the world before cell phones? Unless you were one of the few people with a car phone, you couldn't check in with anyone. If you were picking someone up from the airport or meeting someone, it needed to be well coordinated. You could call someone only if they had a phone at home, at the workplace, or the building where they happened to be at the time.

One of the things I used to do early on in our marriage was hide notes in Mark's briefcase or his sock drawer. They were just little surprises for him to find that let him know that I loved him or I was thinking about him. It was fun to see how much he liked it. Words really do have power to demonstrate love.

I would still recommend writing notes, even in a world of smartphones. But texting (unless you're driving, of course) can be a great way to send a much-needed note to the most important person in your life. And in a world where many couples travel for work, texting can be a great way to stay connected throughout the day.

If you want to inflate your husband's heart like a balloon, then take this challenge. It's simple! Just send him ten texts over the next ten days. Either create your own or use the ones below.

1. **Just wanted you to know that you are on my mind today. I'm your #1 fan and cheering you on. Go get 'em!**

2. **Did you know that I love you more today than the day we got married? I really do.**

3. **I appreciate your hard work and tenacity even though I may not say it often enough.**

4. **If there were more men like you in this world, it would be a better place. And I hope our kids grow up to be just like you.**

5. **If you feel really burdened today, remember that I want to help you and I am praying for you.**

6. I miss you and I'm looking forward to having some time alone with you soon. Let's plan on something!

7. I am so proud to be your wife. You are so good at _____.

8. If you asked me again today, even after all we've been through, I'd still say, "I do!"

9. I appreciate that you try to show me you love me in different ways. Thanks for _____, it made me feel so good.

10. The day's been rough, the week's been long, but I'm still so glad we're in this adventure together. I love you.

TAKING THE NEXT STEP

- This can be an easy experiment. Start texting today, either one or several a day.
- What kind of response did your husband have with each text? Which did he seem to like the best?

_____

_____

5 Things Your Husband Should Expect You to Be

After we got married, we discovered our differing gifts and divvied up household responsibilities according to those gifts. For example, I am the financial person, so I am expected to pay the bills. Mark likes to fix things when they are broken, especially if I validate him afterward. So when stuff around the house needs repairing I expect him to fix it. These are just a few of the expectations we have negotiated in our marriage.

While personalities, responsibilities, and many other things will differ from marriage to marriage, there are reasonable, nonnegotiable marriage expectations that should be the same for all wives. So here are five things your husband should expect you to be. Remember: Each is a way you demonstrate your love for him.

1. Respectful.

You may see the word *respect* and immediately shut down because you feel you have a husband unworthy of respect.

Respect doesn't mean that you have to like or agree with everything he says or does. But it is possible to disagree respectfully, honoring him and his opinions even if you think differently. Cutting, condescending comments or rolling of the eyes punch a hole in the respect tank. I am guilty of this one most of all.

One of a guy's greatest needs is for reassurance that he has what it takes. In fact, in his best-seller, *Love & Respect: The Love She Most Desires, The Respect He Desperately Needs*, Dr. Emerson Eggerichs says that this kind of affirmation is the number one fuel a man needs in his marriage. Without it, he can grind to a halt.

2. Trustworthy.

We talked about the importance of trust and how to build it in List 5. Transparency in marriage must be like a pane of glass—you can see in from both sides. So just as husbands need to be completely honest and true to their words, so do their wives. In our marriage, we can check up on all our computer and phone activities at any time. We are committed not only to being honest about what we do, but also about how we feel. We do not keep secrets from each other. At the same time, there are some secrets women should consider holding—those about their husbands. Friendships with other ladies are important to women, but your husband shouldn't be made to feel unduly "exposed" by what you talk about when you're with them.

3. Faithful.

Fidelity and purity are required in every marriage. Hearts and minds must be guarded. Sexual temptation isn't an issue only for men. More women are becoming addicted to Internet porn as it proliferates. While that online lure may not affect you, there are still the cyberdangers of social media—in the shape of an old school boyfriend or guy you follow on Facebook. You secretly admire the way they talk to and talk about their wives and their families; if only your husband was the same way. For some women, emotional infidelity is much more of a temptation than a physical affair—and it can be easier to hide.

And sometimes unfaithfulness isn't a blatant decision but a consequence of other choices, kind of by default. In the busyness of life, juggling work and children and church, your husband can lose out on your affections. The result is that the person who should be first in your life gets dropped to the bottom of the list. That's a subtle form of unfaithfulness.

4. A helper.

Acknowledging your husband's role as leader of your family does not mean that he is a dictator and you are a doormat. It means that he has a huge responsibility to love you and serve you and your children well. Furthermore, being a helper suggests you are enabling him to achieve something he cannot manage on his own.

In some ways, a leader can be only as good as those who follow. How are you enabling your husband to grow as a leader? Do you welcome his initiative, bringing your insights to help develop a shared vision for your life together—for your family? Do you bring your strengths to supplement his areas of weakness? Or are you questioning his judgment and resisting his efforts to fulfill the role God has given him?

5. Sexually intimate.

Anyone who has been married for some length of time knows that physical intimacy does not always involve candlelight and passion. Sometimes it's about commitment and fulfilling physical desires. When kids come along and life gets crazy-busy, it may be necessary to plan for specific times of intimacy.

God instructs husbands and wives that their bodies are not their own and that they need to meet their partner's needs. Yet we are wired so differently. Women commonly find that emotional connection is the pathway to sex while for guys it's often the other way around—sex leads to emotional closeness. Recognizing this means that sometimes you'll welcome your husband's desire for you, even if you are *not in the mood*.

TAKING THE NEXT STEP

- How well are you meeting these expectations? Give yourself a report card in each subject (grades A to F).

____ Respectful

____ Trustworthy

____ Faithful

____ Helper

____ Sexually Intimate

- Where do you need to improve and why?

_____

_____

~~~

8 Expectations for a Great Marriage

Friends of ours went on a river-rafting trip in Colorado. The company they went with had a guide mounted in the middle of each boat with oars on either side. Most of the rafts had guides who were big, strong guys. Their guide was Suzy, a petite blonde girl in her early twenties. Any rafting trip begins with a calm river that eventually leads to rapids. At the time of the trip, the owner came and warned the guides to avoid shooting one of the rapids straight on and to stay to the side. He looked directly at Suzy and she just smiled behind her Ray-Bans.

During the course of the rafting trip, they noticed that the strong male guides in the other boats were straining to keep their boats steady. One boat even got into trouble and needed assistance. Meanwhile Suzy wasn't even breaking a sweat. She would command the crew when to stroke and make only an occasional stroke herself. Eventually, they hit the forbidden rapid. The other boats began to wade to the right, but not Suzy. She calmly began to dictate orders one after another, instructing her team through a wall of water that they couldn't even see the other side of. And then it was over—they had gone straight through without losing control for a second. The big difference between Suzy and the other guides was that she knew the river and she knew what was ahead. She knew what to expect and how to put the boat in the best position to navigate the rapids.

In marriage, knowing what to expect is vitally important. In the early stages of marriage things may seem calm, but often, very quickly, you can hit turbulent waters. Knowing what is ahead in marriage is necessary to navigate those rapids well. This isn't a complete list by any means but here are some things that can be expected in most marriages. We don't want you to be overwhelmed by what could happen; you just need to be prepared for challenges that will likely arise. When they do, it won't mean it's the end of the world, or your marriage.

1. Expect conflict.

Conflict will happen, and that's okay, *if* you handle conflict in a loving, calm way.

2. Expect delays.

Planning for your future is a great thing to do as a couple. Just understand that things don't always arrive on schedule—not babies, not raises, not health problems, not the sitter.

3. Expect disappointments.

File this in the "you're both only human" category. As hard as your husband may try, he will never be perfect. He will fall short of your expectations at some point, and if your expectation of him is to make your world perfect, he won't be able to do that. He also won't be a mind reader, nor will he anticipate all your needs. Don't let your disappointment dull your passion for him.

4. Expect to be annoyed.

What was once appealing is now annoying. Be ready for that habit of his you found so adorable while you were dating to become annoying. But remember this: There are things you're doing that are likely annoying your husband, too. Cut him some slack and continually focus on his good qualities. If you just can't overlook what's bothering you, talk about it in a loving, kind way.

5. Expect to think you're doing more.

You may feel like you're doing more dishes, more laundry, more bedtime reading with the kids, more yard work, more taking the garbage out. You get the idea. When you start feeling put out and put upon, take some time to assess the situation. Then, instead of attacking your husband and demanding more help, sit down and calmly express your desire to do your jobs well, and ask for help.

6. Expect to disagree with some of your husband's decisions.

Just because you are one in marriage doesn't mean you will agree on everything. And, guess what? That's okay. Respect his right to have a different opinion than you. Don't shoot down ideas automatically. There is often more than one way to get the job done.

7. Expect not to be attracted to your husband.

This may never happen to you. You may go through your entire marriage being passionately attracted to your husband. But if, at some point, you're just not that into him, pray that you will have a loving heart and stoke the embers so your fire will burn bright once again.

8. Expect to be with your husband until the end.

This is a mental safety net. Even when you're furious or extremely disappointed with your husband, you will not think of leaving. You can't, remember? You're with him until the end. This expectation also helps you realize that you should work to make your marriage the best it can be, because you are in it for the long haul.

TAKING THE NEXT STEP

- Which of these expectations has been the biggest challenge in your marriage?

  _____

  _____

- Which of these do you feel like you can begin to address today and what will you do? For example, if you feel like you are doing all of the housework, laundry, and cooking, sit down with your husband and let him know calmly that you need help. Figure out a schedule together and divide up the chores.

  _____

  _____

LIST 17

❧

10 Things You Should Never Say to Your Husband

Words. I have said so many I regret. And you can't take them back—that is the problem with words. They have the power to inflict pain for as long as a person can remember them.

A gentle tongue is a tree of life, but perverseness in it breaks the spirit.

—Proverbs 15:4

When we adopted our son he was nine years old. He had never been to school. Every day he had been forced to stay at the orphanage with the preschoolers while the other kids went to school. They told him he was stupid. He believed them. It took me two years to teach him to read, because he wouldn't even try. The words he heard had broken his spirit. I often wonder what would have become of him had he stayed there and never learned what is now one of his greatest passions—to read.

In the movie *The Help* a similar scene plays out. Little Mae Mobley's mom speaks words of defeat into her young ears every day. Aibileen, the children's caretaker, tries to counteract the destructive words. Her gentle tongue repeats to Mae over and over, "You is kind, you is smart, and you is important."

This lesson on how we use words does not pertain just to children. The words we speak have power over our husbands, too. They can be a tree of life or they can break the spirit.

As I've shared before, words have always been important to Mark. There are definitely things I have said to him that I never should have said. Below is a list of those words that have come straight from my mouth or from the mouths of some of my friends. Some are words of habit that I am still trying to control. Some may not seem all that devastating to you, but many of our words are made worse by the tone we use when we say them.

1. "Why would you do that?"

A man feels unsupported when his wife always questions his judgment. A husband needs his wife to value and trust his opinions and decisions even if they prove to be wrong sometimes. That means not constantly questioning his knowledge by saying, "Why do you say that?" or challenging his decisions.

2. "Can't you do anything right?"

A man wants his wife to believe in him and his abilities. Deep down most men question whether or not they measure up. Most of that, right or wrong, is based on what they are able to accomplish. A wife has a powerful influence on whether he feels like he measures up or not. Saying this will confirm his deep insecurity.

3. "I told you so."

Nobody likes to be reminded when they did something wrong, but this phrase adds a new twist to that relationship dagger. It communicates not only that the husband was wrong about something, but seemingly declares just how right she is about something. It's a belittling and demeaning phrase that may serve to make her feel better about herself and her own judgment, but pulls down her husband in the process.

4. "We need to talk."

As necessary as this phrase may be to convey the urgency of a topic, it's usually seen as a signal that either the husband has done something wrong or something really serious has happened. It's not the best way to broach a serious subject. It also can come across as demeaning. Perhaps a better way to accomplish this is to put it in the form of a question like "Can we talk sometime tonight about something important?" or "When would be a good time today for us to catch up on some things?"

5. "I just don't love you anymore. I want a divorce."

What words can wound more than these? And yet so often people think "love" is just an emotion. The *D* word should never be used in marriage. Once these words are spoken, they cannot be taken back. With help, a couple can heal this kind of hurt, but why go there in the first place?

6. "Forget it... I'll just do it myself."

When a wife says this to a husband, she is making him feel incompetent. She's really saying to him, "I don't believe you can do this nearly as well as I can." It invokes all of the feelings of item number 2.

7. "You need to calm down."

Saying this to a man who may already be fired up is like adding gasoline to the fire.

8. "I should never have married you in the first place."

When a wife says this to her husband, she's saying that he is to blame for all of their marriage problems. That everything is his fault.

9. "Why can't you be more like...?"

When saying things like "Why can't you be more like John?" what you're really communicating to him is "You don't make the grade...you're not good enough as a husband."

10. "That's just like you."

This is great if it's said after a success. Unfortunately, most of the time this is said after he messes up. When a wife says this, she is defining her husband in a negative way.

TAKING THE NEXT STEP

- Have you ever used one or more of these phrases? If so, which one caused the most damage?

  _____

  _____

- What other phrases have you said that cause more hurt than help in your marriage?

  _____

  _____

- When your husband is upset, which phrases or attitudes tend to calm or encourage him?

  _____

  _____

LIST 18

7 Things You Should Stop Doing to Your Husband in Public

When our kids were younger, we went to Disney World with another family who had kids the same age as ours. After eight hours in the heat, my friend was clearly struggling. Then one of her kids fell and skinned his knee. While holding the crying little boy, she told her husband to go into the diaper bag to get the Band-Aids. He got the bag and started looking, but couldn't find them. The longer it took him to find the Band-Aids the more her frustration grew.

Finally, she said harshly one of those phrases we talked about in List 17: "Can't you do anything right?" Then she grabbed the bag and continued, "I have to do everything."

She shouldn't have been speaking to him like that to

begin with, but the fact that it was in public made it even worse. Now, I am not innocent. There have been plenty of times where I have been critical of Mark in public and it hurt him. Perhaps you are doing things *in public* that are harming your husband and hurting your marriage. If you are doing any of the following it is time to make a change.

1. Stop criticizing your husband to others.

Being critical of your husband hurts his reputation. It damages whatever respect others have for you, too. And it conveys that your marriage is not a safe place for your husband to be himself.

2. Stop making your husband the punch line.

This behavior belittles him and suggests that you don't care, even if you do. At some point, your husband and others have to wonder, *Are the jokes really jokes?*

3. Stop sharing the details of your love life.

When you share with your girlfriends details of your sex life, it's really breaching trust with your husband. Intimacy is built on trust. When you expose your private love life in your marriage to public scrutiny, especially in a derogatory fashion, you can easily destroy trust.

4. Stop treating your husband like a child.

We've also heard women in public instructing and ordering their husbands around as if they were children. When my kids were little, this was an easy habit for me to fall into. I would instruct the kids on where to go and what to do and just include him in my list of orders.

5. Stop checking out men who aren't your husband.

You may have heard someone say, "I can look at the menu as long as I don't order." That's wrong thinking. Your wandering eyes and careless words may cause your husband to feel insecure, inadequate, and without value.

6. Stop constantly correcting and contradicting your husband.

When your husband is telling a story, stop interrupting to inject missing parts or correct mistakes. I love to tell stories and have often been guilty of interrupting Mark and correcting his side of the story. It tends to deflate him and after a while he will just give up and let me take over. I have to remind myself that it just isn't considerate to interrupt and contradict.

7. Stop flaunting your body to others.

This applies to men and women. Our culture does not value modesty, and when you flaunt your features, it appears as if you're advertising yourself or are available to others. Dress like you're available only to one person— your husband. Because that's the only person you should be available to.

TAKING THE NEXT STEP

* Put a checkmark next to any one you have done.

____ Criticize him

____ Make him the punch line

____ Share intimate details

____ Treat him like a child

____ Check out other men

____ Correct and contradict

____ Flaunt your body

* How does it affect your husband? How does it affect him when you do the opposite?

_____

_____

* Why do you think you do any of the above?

_____

_____

* Ask your husband: What is one thing you wish I would change about the way I talk about you to others?

_____

LIST 19

What to Do When You're Not in the Mood

When you have kids, employees, and friends to serve and love, it can be hard to have enough energy left over to love your husband well. Yet of all the people I love, Mark is the one I care about and want to please most. So I've had to figure out how to make Mark a priority when I'm tired, distracted by the kids, and flat-out not in the mood.

The most important step in making Mark a priority is to remind myself of his rank—I love Mark first, more than the kids, work, friends, and everything and everyone but God. I love him first and foremost. I just don't always think about it. I take him for granted as a partner in marriage and parenting, instead of making him a priority—a physical priority! If you are like me and you're ready to take steps toward putting your spouse and your marriage first, here are three things to do when you don't feel like having sex:

1. Have sex anyway.

My husband loves it when I show him physical affection. It is his only love language—one of the main ways he feels cared for by me. So saying no to intimacy means I'm not loving him well in that moment. He ends up feeling rejected as a man and disconnected.

Some of you may be thinking, "Well, I can't just pretend to want sex to make him happy!" And this is true. But if you love him and want to please him, it is not pretending. It looks something like this: "You know, honey, I'm really tired tonight and I'd rather do it in the morning. But I hear you, and I want to love you well. So let's do it tonight." This way, you aren't pretending, but you're choosing to find joy in putting his happiness before your own.

2. Get in the mood.

If you're still worried about not wanting to pretend to enjoy sex when you don't really want it, then I have four words for you: Get in the mood! Send the kids to bed early, light candles, put on some music, and turn the lights down low. If romance is what you need, then do whatever it takes to put some romance in the air. Realistically, we have to realize that not every time we have sex will be magical. Not every time will have fireworks. But every time is still a chance to love your spouse well and become more connected with him.

3. Save time and energy for him—the love of your life.

There have been plenty of times when I've been too tired to be physically intimate. It's late at night when I finally fall into bed, and I want more than anything to just close my eyes and drift off into dreamland. But then I see my husband next to me, wide awake and ready to hold me close...and I feel awful that I can't stay awake. Over the years, I've come to understand the importance of saving time and energy for my husband. When I go-go-go between my job, kids, and housework, I'm completely spent by the end of the day. So if I really want my relationship with my husband to continue growing, then I have to intentionally save time and effort to make sexual intimacy with him a priority.

And if I save time and energy, I usually don't have a problem getting in the mood!

TAKING THE NEXT STEP

- What does it take for you to get in the mood?

  _____

  _____

- What gets in the way of you wanting or enjoying sex?

  _____

  _____

- What can you do to put your husband's needs before your own? For example, if your husband is always the one who initiates sex, then commit to making the first move tonight.

  _____

  _____

LIST 20

6 Ways to Push Your Husband Away

It's so easy to push your spouse away. And you can do so without even realizing it.

On several occasions, I've pushed Mark away. The biggest way I have done it is by taking him for granted, as I've said before. I like to commit myself to a lot of different things, particularly if our children are involved. I need a twelve-step program for how to stop volunteering for things. "Hi, my name is Susan and I can't say no." In all seriousness, Mark ends up getting pushed to the back burner. It's not intentional, but it still has the same damaging effect.

You may not push your husband away intentionally, but there are six things you may be doing that are keeping him at a distance.

1. Too much screen time—computer, TV, phone.

Posting, commenting, shopping, watching, gaming, chatting, texting, e-mailing, downloading, blogging, calling, reading, researching—there's a ton of things to do on our computers and smartphones. Much of it is good, but too much of a good thing can be bad sometimes, especially when it takes priority over spending time with your husband. I am guilty of being on my phone a lot and not being present with Mark when it's time for the two of us to spend time together. So turn it off, power it down, and put it away.

2. Hyperscheduling.

I'm really busy right now. Most of us have likely said those words recently. It's probably true. Our calendars are simply filled to the brim. Sure, there are some things on your schedule that you really can't practically control, but there are many things that you *can* control. Remember this: Your busy schedule plus your husband's busy schedule equals missed opportunities to enjoy life and each other. So start saying no to more things outside the home and saying yes to more things inside. Set a date night each week with your husband to spend one-on-one time together.

3. Good-gone-bad habits.

Cleaning the house, working, playing sports, hobbies, or even exercising are all good things. If, however, they become habits that you just can't stop, then they are good things in your life gone bad. If you simply can't go to bed with your husband because the house isn't clean. Or if you have to play eighteen holes of golf every Saturday with the girls. Or if you haven't taken a vacation because you can't leave work. Then your relationship with your spouse may very well suffer, because you have filled his priority spot with something else.

4. Avoiding intimacy.

We talked about this in List 19. It is important enough to repeat. When you and your spouse got married, you became "one flesh." You were designed to enjoy one another emotionally and physically. Sexual intimacy is a wonderful gift, and it should not be withheld as punishment or used to manipulate your husband.

5. Financial irresponsibility.

Fifty-seven percent of couples cite money issues as the number one reason behind their divorces. Unbridled spending and debt can cause huge stress in a marriage. Start a budget. Don't spend more than you've got. If you feel the urge to hide what you spent, that feeling should be a red flag that tells you it was wrong. Spending and lying can create a lot of distrust that will push your husband away.

6. Keeping a list of wrongs.

Do you keep a constant running tab in your mind of how your husband has hurt you and failed you? It's hard to let the hurts go. If not dealt with, that list of wrongs will eventually become a list of resentments moving you to bitterness and then to anger. Seek forgiveness and grant forgiveness to him. If you are having trouble, review List 13.

TAKING THE NEXT STEP

* Is there anything that you do that might push your husband away? Is there anything in the list above?

_____

_____

* Choose one to work on this week. Do the opposite of that thing that pushes him away. For example, if you keep a mental list of all of the ways he has hurt you, then write down a list of all of the ways he has loved you well. For another example, if you overvolunteer, make a list of all of the things you are involved in, rate their importance, and cut out the less important ones from your schedule.

LIST 21

8 Creative Ways to Flirt with Your Husband

When Mark was a senior in high school he was voted Most Flirtatious. His school didn't even have that superlative—they created it for him. These days he doesn't flirt with anyone but me. I not only appreciate it, I would be offended otherwise. The point is, he is good at flirting with me. I'm not that great at it.

Flirting, by definition, is playfully communicating sexual interest or attraction to someone. And flirting with your husband can reap lots of benefits. Flirting can communicate that you still find your husband desirable. It can create more intimacy with him. Flirting in front of your kids, even though they may react with something like "That's gross," will reinforce a sense of love and stability at home as they see their parents showing a healthy desire to be with each other.

So here are eight playful, fun, and creative ways to flirt with your husband.

1. Give him the look.

You can do this anywhere. Raise your eyebrows just a little and give him the once-over when you know he can see you. In a restaurant, in your bathroom, at the breakfast table over the kids' heads, in church, anywhere and everywhere.

2. Give him some lip.

Kiss, kiss, kiss in the morning, at night, in front of the kids, in front of his friends, in front of his coworkers, in front of his family. Nothing makes Mark blow up with pride more than when his wife can't keep her lips off of his.

3. Give him some chatter.

Tell him you like his hair, his eyes, his hands, his shirt, his biceps, his brain. You like the way he drives, fixes the toilet, makes your coffee, mows the lawn, plays the guitar.

You think he is the most..., best at..., smartest in..., helpful with...

You got the picture?

4. Give him the tease.

I love this and think it can be wickedly fun. Tease him when you know it can't go any further. For example, when you are sitting side by side at a long, boring dinner or banquet somewhere. Play with his hands under the table by writing on his palm, sitting up against him, whispering a couple things in his ear. It will entertain him and make him crazy.

5. Give him a creative thought.

Have you ever heard the SHMILY story? It's the story about a couple who had an ongoing competition to write SHMILY (See How Much I Love You) to each other in creative ways. For example, in lipstick on the mirror, in shoe polish on the car window, in flour on the kitchen counter. Come up with an original acronym. One I use for our family is LYLACCC (Love You Like A Chocolate Chip Cookie).

6. Give him a peek.

You are married! His body is yours and yours is his. I am a flannel pajama girl, but I have lots of friends who take advantage of prettier things for their husband's benefit.

7. Give him a romantic night out.

You need this just as much as he does. Plan it, prepare for it, save for it, and make it a memory. Go old-school and relive early romantic days, or make it an adventure and try something new. Create a bucket list of ideas and go out often.

8. Give him a romantic night in.

If you are out of money or out of babysitters, create a night in. Spread a picnic under the stars in the backyard. Make a scavenger hunt that ends in the bedroom. In fact, the best thing about a night in is that the bedroom is only seconds away!

There are many ways you can show your husband you are still into him after all these years. Find what works for you. One final thought: Even if your kids act grossed out, you're not only showing them you are into their dad, but you're also setting their expectations for how to be a healthy, flirtatious spouse someday.

TAKING THE NEXT STEP

- Whatever you did with your husband when you first started dating worked, because he married you! Think back: In what ways would you flirt with him? In what ways would he flirt with you?

  _____

  _____

- Flirt with your husband today. Do what you used to do or try some of the suggestions above. If you have kids, have fun with it and enjoy grossing them out!

LIST 22

6 Things You Must Know About Your Husband

The earlier you learn these things the better. As I have said, when we first started having kids, Mark was sometimes critical of me. It seemed like every week his criticism would change, and I always felt as if I was failing to meet his expectations. We could not resolve our problem on our own and invested in marriage counseling. It was one of the best investments we have ever made, and I highly recommend it.

Our counselor was able to objectively identify clear solutions to our problem. We needed to be realistic about our needs and expectations. (Hopefully, you are reaping the benefit of all we learned as we have focused on expectations in many of the chapters in this book!) The counselor was able to drill down for both of us what was really important for Mark. She had him rank all the things he had asked of me over the years. Then she asked, "If there was just one thing that I could execute well for him during this busy season of young children, what would it be? And if I promised to do it well, could he be content?"

He chose physical intimacy, regularly and often. She asked me to commit to that as his standard and I did. Then she asked him to let go of everything else and to be grateful to have that. Physical intimacy is Mark's love language. So I started giving him more of that, and it worked. He was able to let other things go.

It is not easy to understand your spouse. Becoming one is an ongoing process. I needed to know Mark's priority, and Mark needed to understand my limitations. In this list you will find six things you must know to better understand your husband.

1. What is his love language?

Gary Chapman's classic book *The 5 Love Languages: The Secret to Love That Lasts* explains how we receive and "hear" love in different ways: receiving gifts, quality time, words of affirmation, acts of service, and physical touch. Which of these say, "I love you" to him the most? And remember that he may be using the same style to communicate his love to you, without realizing you may "hear" it differently. Perhaps he is telling you he loves you in ways you miss.

2. What is his biggest dream?

In his book *Wild at Heart*, John Eldredge says every man wants an adventure to live. What is your husband's? Does he long to start his own business or scale the highest peak on every continent? Has he buried his deepest desires in the duty of everyday responsibilities? Are there some ways you can help reawaken or encourage him in reaching for a brave goal that will stretch his faith?

3. What spells romance for him?

Anything that ends up with physical intimacy, you may be thinking. That's certainly an element, most likely, but men like to be pursued, too. When you turn the tables and do the pursuing, it can make him feel that he has still got it. Initiating says that you are not just willing to respond to his advances but want to make your own. When did you last make plans and invite him out on a date?

4. What does he enjoy doing?

How does he like to spend time when he's not fulfilling responsibilities at work or around the home or in the family? There is a good chance it will be activity-based somehow, whether it's working in the garage or cheering on a team. Do you help create room and time for his hobbies and interests, within reason, or do you view them as competition? Remember, when he is recharged, he has more to bring back to you.

5. What makes him feel valued?

In the movie *The Intern*, Robert De Niro plays a seventy-year-old retiree applying for an internship. In his application video he says, "I just want to be needed again." Guys need to know that they are needed, that their contribution is important, not just their paycheck. Do you thank him verbally? Leave him the occasional appreciative note?

6. What does he struggle with most in your marriage?

While the area of your relationship that most concerns you is probably no secret to him, chances are he may not be so forthcoming about what bothers him. He may not want to rock the boat or risk conflict, or he truly may not even have thought about it; as far as he is concerned, everything is fine. But he may welcome an invitation to talk nonconfrontationally about things. You could ask each other what would help you enrich your marriage, opening the door for a deeper conversation.

TAKING THE NEXT STEP

* Test yourself about your husband. Answer these six questions how you think your husband will answer. Then have him answer them. Check your answers. How many are a match?

	Your Answers	*His Answers*
Love Language	_____	_____
	_____	_____
Biggest Dream	_____	_____
	_____	_____
Romance	_____	_____
	_____	_____
Feeling Valued	_____	_____
	_____	_____
Enjoys Doing	_____	_____
	_____	_____
Biggest Struggle	_____	_____
	_____	_____

- Did any of his answers surprise you?

  _____

  _____

- How often do you spend time creating space so he can do his favorite thing? What is something you can sacrifice to make sure he is able to do it?

  _____

  _____

6 Things to Do When You're Lonely in Marriage

As humans, we are not meant to be isolated. We all crave deep and lasting connections with other people. But we know it's possible to feel alone in the middle of a crowd, and it's possible to sleep in the same bed with a spouse for years and still feel lonely. Many of us never expect to be lonely in marriage, each hoping that our husband will be the lifelong companion who saves us from loneliness. Over time, however, couples can gradually disconnect from one another and find themselves feeling isolated and withdrawn.

Loneliness is not just about physical proximity, it's about emotional connection. FamilyLife's Dr. Dennis Rainey and his wife, Barbara, explain: "You may have sex, but you don't have love. You may talk, but you don't communicate. You live together, but you don't share life." If you're feeling lonely in your marriage, here are some ways to reconnect with your husband.

1. Make the first move.

Feelings of loneliness are seldom felt by only one person in a relationship. If you're feeling isolated, chances are your husband is, too. Take the first step to reconnecting with him, even if it's just a small gesture. Open up to him about how you feel and give him an opportunity to do the same. Healing cannot begin if you hide or mask your pain.

2. Forgive past hurts.

Especially if you have been feeling alone for a long time, hurts have likely been building up in your marriage. Nothing breeds loneliness more than unforgiven hurt and conflict. If you have been wronged, make the decision to forgive your husband. And if you have wounded him, seek his forgiveness immediately.

3. Spend time together.

This seems like a no-brainer, but sometimes couples get so busy or caught up in their individual lives that they neglect to simply spend time together. The less time a couple spends together, the more likely they are to feel distant from each other. This can be resolved by deliberately scheduling date nights in, date nights out, TV-free nights, and occasional weekend getaways—just for the two of you.

4. Make your time count.

The quantity of time together is really important, but so is the quality of that time. Couples have to be intentionally focused on their time together to create a marital connection. When you and your husband are talking, put down your cell phone, set aside distractions, and focus on each other. Find ways to bond over shared experiences: taking a walk, cooking dinner, going to a concert or sporting event, or playing a board game or cards together. Encourage and compliment your husband. Make your moments together count.

5. Prioritize physical closeness.

This is not just referring to sexual intimacy, though that is certainly an important part of marital closeness, but also to the little things that may have fallen by the wayside, like holding hands or snuggling on the couch. The key to resurrecting physical touch is to start small. Sit close to each other, give neck massages, and pull out a surprise kiss.

Getting closer physically will naturally lead to feeling closer emotionally.

6. Don't be afraid to ask for help.

While the idea of seeking outside input for your marriage can be intimidating, nearly every couple can benefit from good marriage counseling. Getting an outside perspective can be extremely helpful to you and your husband.

You may feel lonely in your marriage, but you are not alone in the struggle for marital intimacy. We have all experienced loneliness in our lives, but you don't have to feel it in your marriage.

TAKING THE NEXT STEP

- Have you ever felt lonely in your marriage? If so, what have you done about it?

_____

_____

- What can you do to reconnect with your husband? Which one of the above suggestions will you commit to today?

_____

_____

LIST 24

5 Ways to Use Body Language to Connect

I've always been able to read Mark's body language and facial expressions. However, I've watched how others get confused and misread him at work in particular. When Mark focuses on something, he gets very intense. His eyebrows get furrowed and his facial muscles tighten. Most people think he looks angry, but he's really not. I've seen others, including our children, misread his body language and react by being intimated or blowing up.

Our nonverbals communicate just as much as our spoken words. Sometimes it is easy to see, but many times it is subtle and takes a trained eye. Understanding body language will help you avoid breakdowns in communication with your husband. Becoming an expert in postures, arm motions, and facial expressions can save hurt feelings and enhance communication in your marriage. Understanding your husband's body language will also show him how much you care. Take a look at how you can use your body language to connect with your husband.

1. Use your eyes.

The eyes are a lamp to the soul. Making eye contact shows that you are engaged and interested. Looking away occasionally communicates that you are processing what he is saying. However, if you look away and off into the distance a lot, more than likely you are going to give him the impression that you are not paying attention. He'll feel as though you don't care. If either of you are looking at the ground, it means there are feelings of intimidation, defeat, hurt, or sadness. Rapid blinking denotes someone is feeling uncomfortable or upset. Squinted eyes can communicate sympathy, but they more often send a message of skepticism. Eye rolling is a sarcastic dismissal and should be avoided at all costs.

2. Use your mouth.

Besides the obvious frown and smile, the mouth can reveal quite a bit. Pursed lips, for example, tell him that you either don't approve or trust him—or what he is saying. Biting the lips reveals anxiety or worry. Hands covering the mouth indicates that he is hiding an emotional reaction. It may reveal some insecurity or lack of confidence.

3. Use your hands.

The hands can disarm and draw in, or they can push away and make him defensive. Keeping your hands open is inviting. It says that you are open-minded and ready to hear what he has to say. Never close your fist. It communicates anger and that you are closed off. Be careful when using exaggerated motions with your hand. Sometimes it shows excitement, which can be good in certain situations, but in an argument it escalates the tension.

4. Use your posture.

When thinking about posture, one powerful way to connect is by mirroring. It's making the same pose and forming the same posture as him. Many times we do it naturally without thinking about it. Mirroring powerfully communicates a desire to connect and be on the same page. When you see him strike the same pose, it means you are on the right track. On your part, keep this in mind and consciously do it when you two are having trouble connecting. In a disagreement, stay away from slouching, crossing your arms, and putting your hands on your hips. If you are slouching, it may show that you have checked out. Crossing arms says that you are defensive and closed off. Hands on the hips means you are aggressively challenging him.

5. Use your vocal tones.

Be aware of your volume and pitch. Raising your volume escalates things and shows you are trying to dominate. Lowering your volume can communicate that you are trying to calm things down; however, going too low (close to a mumble) can give off the impression you are withholding or hiding something. A higher pitch shows excitement or irritation, while a lower pitch is more relaxed. During an argument, try to maintain a lower pitch to help defuse things. Be aware of how placing an emphasis on certain words can change the meaning of what you say. Emphasize words of love and understanding.

TAKING THE NEXT STEP

- How has your body language escalated a situation in the past? How has it helped defuse a situation?

  _____

  _____

- How can you change from using negative body language to using positive body language?

  _____

  _____

- When your husband communicates with you, do you feel like you understand his body language, or have you misread him before?

  _____

  _____

LIST 25

10 Ways to Affair-Proof Your Marriage

The slippery slope toward an affair can start quickly, perhaps as a result of significant problems in the relationship, or slowly with a couple drifting apart. A spouse feels neglected and rejected. She doesn't feel like he pays attention to her, or he feels like she is never interested in sex. Someone gets hurt, maybe even repeatedly. The feelings and voices replay over and over again: "He doesn't appreciate me." "She never shows me affection." "He takes me for granted." "She doesn't love me."

Then it happens. While at work or a party, there is an interaction with someone of the opposite sex. The spouse feels good and excited, two things that haven't been felt in a while. That was what happened to a friend of mine. She had daily interactions with another man, and she started to tell him all of the things wrong in her marriage. He had a sympathetic ear. It started as an emotional affair (as is the case with many women), but eventually she had a physical affair and left her husband. The parties involved normally don't intend for it to go that far. It starts small and builds, ultimately ending at a place no one wanted to be.

We must actively protect our marriages. Start by committing yourself to the following practices in order to affair-proof your marriage.

1. Establish guardrails.

Mark and I have a rule, as well as a Family First policy, that we will not travel together alone with a person of the opposite sex. We also avoid intimate conversations about our personal lives with the opposite sex. Many affairs begin when people start talking about their personal pressures and problems with another person besides their husband. That's what happened to my friend. She felt like the other person empathized and understood her better. This can then lead to a feeling of closeness, which, if left unchecked, can lead to an intimate emotional or physical relationship.

2. Stop viewing pornography.

Pornography destroys people and relationships. While it's more often an issue with men, it's no longer just a guy problem. More and more women are viewing pornography too. Porn creates unrealistic and false expectations for your sexual relationship with your husband. It promotes the lie that relationships are all about getting, instead of giving. Another lie about pornography is that "I'll do it one more time, then I'll stop." But some is never enough; you always want more. Pornography is like a drug—you always need more and more and something stronger and stronger for the high to continue. As a result, soft porn leads to hard porn. And pornography often leads to an extramarital affair. So, what should you do? Start by bringing to light what has been hidden in darkness by sharing your struggles with your husband, pastor, or friend. Immediately flee from it and avoid pornography completely. Don't watch it with your husband. Put your computer in a very public place in your house or get rid of it for a season of time. Never erase your computer history. Allow your husband or a friend to hold you accountable.

3. Date your husband.

Have a date night and treat it like a very important appointment by marking it on your calendar. Some people are able to do this every week. You may find that works for you. We find that every other week seems to work better for our schedules. Make your date something fun and interactive. Have dinner at a new restaurant, play tennis, go bowling, go dancing, or take a walk.

4. Fire up the romance.

The best way to avoid a spark with someone else is to keep the home fires burning. It doesn't take much to start the romance. A short love letter takes only a few minutes to write. Putting a sticky note on the mirror telling your husband that you can't wait for your date tonight can work wonders.

5. Be affectionate.

Being playfully affectionate with your husband will also stoke the home fire and will help snuff out any hint of an outside spark. Wink at him across the dinner table, give him big hugs, hold his hand when you're on a date, and cuddle in bed.

6. Enjoy physical intimacy often.

It happens all too often: One spouse starts exploring a sexual relationship outside the home because that desire is not being satisfied in his marriage. Exhaustion, busyness, emotional distance, and many other things cause sexual encounters to wither. While those may be valid reasons, they must be dealt with to the extent possible so that the opportunity for frequent physical intimacy is welcomed in your marriage.

7. Build in couch time each day.

Get into the habit of having time on the couch together without the TV on or other technological distractions. Tell him you would like to spend fifteen minutes each day with him either first thing in the morning, after work, or after the kids go to bed. It may feel forced or awkward at first, but after it becomes a habit it'll just be a normal and rich part of your day.

Ask each other about the day. What was the most stressful? What was the most enjoyable? Saying sweet things to him may get him to open up. Start by telling him how glad you are to see him. Discuss what you've been thinking about lately. It's creating opportunity for connection.

8. Play together.

Playing together creates oneness in marriage. Your play might include collecting things together. Maybe it's antiques.

It could be you introducing him to the theater or him introducing you to fishing. Or find something that's new to both of you. I like to dance, so I'm going to get Mark to take dance classes with me.

9. Speak kind words.

After many years of marriage, sometimes you need to go back to the basics. When you wake up in the morning, say, "Good morning, honey." When you arrive home, ask, "How was your day?" When you go to bed, pray with him and say "I love you" every single night.

10. Worship together.

I'm not just talking about singing, although that is important. Worship is about God being at the center of your life. Just as the earth revolves around the sun and keeps a constant orbit as a result of the gravitational pull of the sun, your life as a couple should constantly, day in and day out, revolve around God. As you attend church, pray, and grow in God together, you'll grow as one. I realize that opening your heart to God in front of your spouse may at first be a bit uncomfortable, but it's worth it. As you pray together, you'll get a front-row seat into one another's soul.

TAKING THE NEXT STEP

- Which one of these suggestions made you uncomfortable or maybe even cringe a little bit (or a lot)? Why do you think it caused a reaction?

  _____

  _____

- Do you feel that you have affair-proofed your marriage? After reading the above, do you see any areas where you may be at risk?

  _____

  _____

- Think about it. What action can you take today to protect your marriage?

  _____

  _____

LIST 26

10 Questions to Ask Your Husband Every Year

We were on a trip with another family who were good friends. The other couple was so sweet to one another in both their affection and their words. We noticed that we really didn't interact in that way. We tended to be more direct with one another, and we wondered a little if there was something wrong with us. We wished we communicated a little more like them.

Soon thereafter, we were shocked when the wife filed for divorce. The husband said he was equally stunned. During the divorce proceedings the judge asked her the reason for her decision. She attempted to justify her actions by saying, "I'm just not happy." While they were sweet and affectionate with one another in public, they clearly weren't talking in private. Somewhere the pursuit of continually getting to know one another had stopped. They became disconnected.

Good conversations lead to connection and intimacy. The best way to facilitate a good conversation is to ask great questions. Whether you feel like you know your husband well or not, the questions below will be helpful. The woman who becomes an expert in the art of asking questions is the woman who will win her husband's heart. Ask your husband these ten questions every year (or more often, if you'd like).

1. What are you enjoying most about our relationship right now?

Talking about what is going right will create optimism and renew energy. Tell him what you enjoy most about him.

2. What has been your biggest surprise in the last year?

This is a great way to gain insight into his expectations and the things he considers most important.

3. Where would you like our relationship to be this time next year?

It doesn't matter where you are, there's always room to be better. He might say, "I'd like to see more spontaneous intimacy." Or, "I want us to be moving forward together in our faith." He could say, "I want our relationship to involve more fun!"

4. How are you feeling about life in general?

Never assume you know how he is feeling. He may look okay on the surface but be overwhelmed underneath. Don't just listen to what he says, but be sure to read between the lines as well.

5. What are your dreams for our future?

If you want to know what gets him up in the morning and what gives him hope, it's going to be this one. Find out his highest hopes for your future together. Give him the time to paint the picture for you.

6. If you could go anywhere, where would you go?

Encourage him to fantasize about his ideal vacation. Get excited and dream with him. Maybe someday you can surprise him and make it a reality.

7. How do you think we're doing financially?

This needs to be an ongoing conversation. Just like a board of directors of a business meets annually to have a comprehensive meeting to evaluate the finances and the plan for the coming year, a husband and wife should do the same.

8. What do you want to do this year to improve our health?

Being in shape and eating well gives you more energy in everyday life. Encourage one another to exercise. It is a great activity to do together. Explore creative cooking and focus on food that makes you feel good.

9. What is one thing you would change about how our family relates to one another?

This is one to brainstorm together. Set a vision of what a healthy family looks like, then model it. A few examples could be less TV, more constructive communication with less yelling, getting time away together, or eating dinner together more.

10. What is one thing I give my time to that you think would be better spent somewhere else?

You need to know where he wants your time. This will give him an open door to ask for it. It's an opportunity to see what he thinks is important.

TAKING THE NEXT STEP

- Think back to before you were married, when you and your husband were dating. Do you remember a conversation that could have lasted all night? What made it that way?

  _____

  _____

- What can you do to spark that interest again? Which one of these questions would be a great place to start today?

  _____

  _____

~

7 Things to Avoid When Fighting with Your Husband

Mark and I handle conflict very differently. He is an attorney, so right off the bat he is tough to argue with. His memory is phenomenal. Early in our marriage I wouldn't be able to get a word in, and so I would shut down when we had an argument. That would make him even more mad. We've had to work on those habits and change.

Another difference is that when an issue arises I have to speak about it right then. There have been times when Mark is heading to a speaking engagement and I will bring up an issue with him on the phone. Once I get it out there, I'm fine and I can let it go. But Mark reacts differently. He will stew about the can of worms I just opened for hours. Several times I've sent him off on the wrong foot to some of his public speaking engagements, because I couldn't wait.

How we communicate with our husbands and respond to them is critical to our relationship. The best way is through an assertive style of honesty, grace, and love. The assertive person deals directly, honestly, and, most important, *respectfully* with others about what they are thinking and feeling.

Unfortunately, arguments typically escalate into communication that is aggressive or passive-aggressive. And when that happens, a husband or wife can use cruel words that hit below the belt, which, in the end, only harms the relationship. This list should help by outlining seven things to avoid when fighting with your husband.

1. You compare your husband to other family members in a negative light.

You're just like your father!

2. You assassinate his character.

You're lazy/inconsiderate/stupid/evil—pretty much any name-calling.

3. You bring up the past even when it was supposedly resolved or forgiven.

As we shared in List 13, when you truly forgive your husband, you release and pardon him from the offense. That means you cannot bring him into the marital courtroom again for that same offense.

4. You bring the kids into it against your husband.

When it comes to an argument between you and your husband, the kids should be off-limits. Children don't understand the nuance, context, and complexities of the issues that their parents argue about. Forcing them to take sides is certainly a slap in the face to your husband and to your children. *You see what your father is like? You see how he treats me?*

5. You don't allow your husband to disagree or get a word in.

Resolving conflict requires each spouse to hear out the other. If you are constantly squelching or putting off discussion, you're really closing off a path to resolution and peace.

6. You shut down completely at the first sign of conflict.

Sometimes a break is needed in the intensity of an argument. But constantly withdrawing from the ring because you don't want to fight can be a low blow as well. Conflict avoidance only delays and compounds the problem. Shutting down is not a long-term solution.

7. You initiate conflict at times or in places where it can't really be dealt with.

In the car, on the way to school or church, in the middle of a store, at a wedding. These are not appropriate places to bring up problems and resolve those big conflicts. Unless you work together to find the right time and place, you risk either embarrassing yourselves by arguing in public or leaving your spouse with no way to properly respond.

TAKING THE NEXT STEP

* In which of the following four ways do you and your husband approach conflict? Why?

You	Your Husband	
_____	_____	Passive: Avoid, avoid, avoid
_____	_____	Aggressive: Attack, control, and provoke
_____	_____	Passive-Aggressive: Surface agreement, secret undermining
_____	_____	Assertive: Honest, direct, clear

* From the above suggestions, what could you do to help make conflict between you and your husband healthier and more productive?

_____

_____

* Ask your husband: What is one thing I do when we are having conflict that you would like me to change?

_____

_____

LIST 28

5 Kinds of Compliments to Give Your Husband

Mark Twain once said, "I can live for two months on a good compliment." I think that's universal. Everyone appreciates a good compliment.

That's *especially* true in marriage. A sincere, timely compliment can be a powerful difference maker for days. Likewise, when you criticize your husband, its effects can be felt for days and even weeks or months. And it's dangerous to mix compliments and criticism, as well.

Increase and improve your compliments to your husband using these five types.

1. Relationship skills: Compliment how he treats you and others.

This type of compliment starts with observing your husband. Note when he shows uncommon kindness, generosity, courtesy, or patience with you or anyone. Say something like "I really admire how kind you were to people in that crazy, crowded store." Or "You are really good at making me feel supported."

2. Parenting skills: Compliment the way he handles your kids.

If he works he can feel less connected to your kids. Your husband is more aware of his parenting mistakes than his parenting strengths. You can help him see what a positive difference he makes in your kids' lives.

3. Get-'er-done skills: Compliment his ability at a task.

It's important to let your husband know that you admire his abilities, but don't just compliment an extraordinary skill. Let him know you appreciate all the things he does by saying, "Thanks for cleaning the kitchen...I was tired and I really appreciated you doing that" or "Thank you for mowing the lawn."

4. Challenges: Compliment his handling of a difficult situation.

If you see your husband navigate a hard situation well, let him know that you noticed. Tell him that you see how he helps your marriage and family. Perhaps say, "I know the last few days were unexpectedly difficult, but we couldn't have made it through without your steady hand. Thanks for keeping us calm."

5. Appearance or style: Compliment the impression he makes on you.

If it's been a long time since you've complimented your husband, unprompted, about his appearance, do it this week.

TAKING THE NEXT STEP

- Write down three things about your husband you could compliment and then share those with him. Note his reaction and observe what types of compliments he enjoys most.

1. _____

2. _____

3. _____

- Compliment Challenge: How many compliments will you give your husband each day this week? Keep track below.

	Sunday	Monday	Tuesday	Wednesday	Thursday	Friday	Saturday
Compliment Count							

~~~

7 Must Dos and Don'ts for Your Marriage

It's often called the Love Chapter, and it's found in the book of 1 Corinthians in the Bible.

Perhaps you've read it, or maybe heard it at a wedding you've attended. Chapter 13, verses 4–7 of that book declare, "Love is patient, love is kind. It does not envy, it does not boast, it is not proud. It is not rude, it is not self-seeking, it is not easily angered, it keeps no record of wrongs. Love does not delight in evil but rejoices with the truth. It always protects, always trusts, always hopes, always perseveres."

Hanging on the wall, these words might be a bright reminder of your special day. Hung in your hearts, they can be a road map to a rich future. Usually, we are told to avoid saying *always* and *never* because they are unhelpful absolutes, but not in this case. This inspiring passage offers wise dos and don'ts that you must embrace for a meaningful, enriching marriage. Let's look at seven of them.

1. Don't be self-seeking.

Most of us like to think of ourselves as nice people—considerate and caring, even—but the reality is that we're all born with a selfish bent. Nothing makes that more apparent than spending your life in close proximity with someone else. Rather than look to your own interests, determine to focus on how you might help your husband by being more loving and giving.

2. Don't be easily angered.

I shared in my book, *The Passionate Mom*, that I can be hot tempered. My temperature can reach a boiling point in seconds flat. Most often my temper is related to my impatience. And my patience is like my car keys; I lose those often, and then I find them in the strangest places. I can lose my patience over silly things and then be superpatient with something else. Identify those things that prompt a knee-jerk reaction in you and try to understand what's going on. Likely it's not so much what your husband actually said or did as some hurt or unresolved issue it's brought out in you.

So don't take it out on him. Better to bite your tongue than to bite his head off.

3. Don't keep a record of wrongs.

Some couples seem to view their relationship a bit like a business arrangement—a series of agreements. If any part of the agreement is not met by one partner, then the other partner has an excuse to do what they want. It's a tit-for-tat kind of relationship. *I am justified in doing this because you did that.* And some of us can use the excuse of "you did that" for decades. Remember that marriage is about giving over getting. Focusing on what you aren't getting is a breeding ground for bitterness. Tear up that mental list of the ways they have let you down. Choose to forgive. Revisiting List 13 will guide you through the process of forgiveness.

4. Do always protect.

Think of your marriage like a field. To harvest a rich crop, you need to take care of it, not only watering and tilling it, but also guarding it against pests and other threats. Like bugs, little things can cause a lot of damage if they are not dealt with. Are you being careful not to let dissatisfaction or temptation gain a foothold? Keep alert to negative outside influences. We talked about ways to affair-proof your marriage in List 25. Constant vigilance is the price of a good marriage.

5. Do always believe the best.

One couple I know included in their vows a pledge I like: "We will assume the best intentions of each other." Remember that you are on the same team, not opponents, even when you may be at odds. Believing the best of and in each other is a helpful perspective to have when there are differences of opinion, maybe even harsh words; it draws you together rather than pushing you apart. If you struggle to believe the best because of past hurts, start by focusing on small ways that he has consistently been there for you.

6. Do always hope.

The right actions are important in marriage, but attitude is critical, too. Chances are that if you don't think things can get better, they probably won't, because you are closing your eyes to the possibilities and opportunities. Forget about your marriage glass being half empty, if that's how you feel, or even half full, for that matter. Instead, concentrate on pouring more of yourself into the glass so that it's filled up.

7. Do always persevere.

A wedding is not about saying "I do" one day. A marriage is about saying "I do" every day, rain or shine, good or bad. You made a promise, you made a commitment. Every marriage will face its challenges; that's a given. You must keep pressing in and pressing forward. That takes intentionality and effort.

TAKING THE NEXT STEP

- Which of these seven dos and don'ts is hardest for you to live out in your marriage right now? Ask your husband which one he thinks you do well.

  _____

  _____

- Choose one to focus on improving over the course of the next week.

  _____

  _____

- Make a list of three ways you think your husband is a good husband. Share it with him.

  _____

  _____

  _____

LIST 30

3 Truths About You

In 1503, a twenty-nine-year-old artist had distinguished himself as the greatest sculptor of his time. He produced works with spectacular detail, the likes of which the world had never seen. His name was Michelangelo. During that time, Michelangelo had a fierce artistic rival named Raphael. In an effort to move attention off of Michelangelo and onto his friend Raphael, a man named Donato Bramante (the original architect of St. Peter's) convinced the Pope to have Michelangelo paint the ceiling of the Sistine Chapel. The strategy was to get Michelangelo away from his most skilled medium, sculpting, and on to painting frescos, where he had no experience.

They underestimated Michelangelo's multidimensional genius as an artist, and the plan backfired. As the noted art historian Giorgio Vasari wrote of Michelangelo's master-piece, the Sistine Chapel ceiling, "The whole world came running when the vault was revealed, and the sight of it was enough to reduce them to stunned silence."

As impressive an artist as Michelangelo was, he pales in comparison to the Master Creator of this world. In fact, it is God who created Michelangelo and his genius. And it is God who created you. You are his masterpiece! You are immeasurably valuable.

In the midst of your hectic schedule, you have sacrificially chosen to read this book because you care about your marriage. I wish I could hug you for caring and for taking many many simple steps to the marriage you want. You have been learning some very important truths about yourself, your husband, and your marriage, because you want to love well.

In Matthew 22:36–39, one of the Pharisees asked Jesus a question to test him:

> "Teacher, which is the greatest commandment in the Law?" And Jesus said to him, "You shall love the Lord your God with all your heart and with all your soul and with all your mind. This is the great and first commandment. And a second is like it: You shall love your neighbor as yourself."

Your husband is your closest neighbor. So as you live out this great commandment of loving your husband well, you are giving joy to the Lord!

In this last list I want to encourage you. I want to remind you that no matter where you are in your relationship with your husband, there is One who loves you perfectly. And I believe He wants you to remember three important truths about yourself.

1. You are valuable for who you are, not for what you do.

You were created exclusively by God and for God. And because of that, you are immeasurably valuable. There were no flaws in your design and no errors in your construction. You are handmade, custom designed, and fully loaded by God.

2. You have gifts—embrace them.

Every person has gifts or strengths that God placed in you for a reason. If you don't know yours, we'd encourage you to ask five family members and friends this question: "In one or two words, what do you think is my single greatest strength?" They'll all probably give you similar answers.

Those answers identifying your area of giftedness will help you understand the truth that you have a lot to offer your family and the world.

3. You weren't meant to do this alone.

If you're constantly putting on a front that you have it all together, other people will start to believe that you really do have it all together. So, we challenge you to be honest with trusted friends and family. Share your struggles with them and let them help carry your burdens and encourage you. Let them love you well! Because the truth is: you were *never* meant to do this alone.

You are valuable. You are gifted. And now you hopefully have the simple steps to love your husband well. You are one with him. Give him 100 percent. Love him for better or for worse. Resist temptation. Pursue holiness. Give even more. Love, love, love, until death do you part.

TAKING THE NEXT STEP

- What good gifts do you bring into your marriage? How does your husband benefit from them? Ask your husband what he thinks your gifts are.

_____

_____

- What gifts does your husband bring to the marriage? How do your differing gifts complement each other?

_____

_____

CONCLUSION: MOVING FORWARD

Congratulations on completing the thirty lists! What you have just accomplished took a great amount of courage and commitment. At the beginning of the book, we told you about our own expectations going into marriage, that we thought it would be easy. We soon realized it was hard work. There have been days where we have made huge gains. There have also been discouraging days where it felt as if we'd moved forward only a little or perhaps even stepped backward. Marriage can be really hard, but remember that God gave you the husband you have. He has called you to love your husband well no matter what. Never stop doing that. Remember, on your deathbed you want to be able to look at yourself and say, "I loved him with everything I am." You want to be confident he knows it. It may take consistency over time before you see results, but it's like Dale Carnegie said: *"Most of the important things in the world have been accomplished by people who have kept on trying when there seemed to be no hope at all."*

So the question is, how did you do? Did you take any steps forward? Did you grow in your love and selflessness? We want to encourage you: Even if you moved only a little bit forward, that is something to feel good about. It means that you have improved as a wife. It means that your husband is more loved today than he was yesterday. We would recommend repeating the process of reading these lists to love by and adding new things to improve upon. We think you'll find yourself gaining momentum as you consistently love your husband well. Now continue forward and build on the work you have started—build your marriage. Taking small steps today will mean getting closer to the marriage you want tomorrow.

ACKNOWLEDGMENTS

The truths in this book are not our own. So we must tell you that the Author of these truths, and all truth, is God Himself. He is truth. And He is worthy of our standing ovation, moment by moment, day by day.

Through our married life, many, many people have spoken into our lives. And while they may not have penned any of the words in this book, we consider them to be co-authors with us. Our children, now all in their twenties, have had a front-row seat in our marriage. Knowing that Megan, Emily, Hannah, Mark Jr., and Grant were always watching inspired us to work really hard in our relationship. And we salute Army Captain Hampton Tignor, who recently married our Megan and now serves our country as a judge advocate general (JAG). You are an inspiration to us. We are also very grateful to our parents for teaching us the importance of family.

We applaud the talented BJ Foster. With great flexibility and ability, BJ spent many hours working with us brainstorming, organizing, and editing the content in this book. And to our team at Family First, we say a big "thank you!" We are honored to stand with you as we strive to be a voice of truth for families.

Once again, we put our hands together for our faithful literary agent, DJ Snell. His gracious style and encouragement have been embraced by us through the process of producing this work.

Joey Paul, Becky Hughes, Patsy Jones, and Andrea Glickson, we shine the spotlight on you and the FaithWords team for your service to us and to all the married couples who, through this book, will be inspired to love one another well.

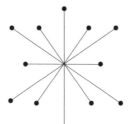

STAY
CONNECTED
Continue the journey to loving well.

CONNECT
with Susan

🌐 BLOG: www.susan.me

📘 facebook.com/susanmerrill

🐦 twitter.com/susan_merrill

📷 instagram.com/susanmerrill

📌 pinterest.com/susan_merrill

READ
Susan's book

📖 *The Passionate Mom—Dare to Parent in Today's World*

CONNECT
with Mark

🌐 BLOG: www.markmerrill.com

📘 facebook.com/markmerrill

🐦 twitter.com/markmerrill

📷 instagram.com/markmerrill

READ
Mark's book

📖 *All Pro Dad—Seven Essentials to Be a Hero to Your Kids*

LISTEN

WATCH

 The Family First Podcast with Mark & Susan Merrill (iTunes)

  Mark and Susan Merrill (YouTube)

EXPLORE
our programs

Mark and Susan are the founders of Family First, a national non-profit organization. The mission of Family First is to provide parenting, marriage and relational truth that helps people love their family well and gives them greater hope for the future. We do this through the following programs.

 All Pro Dad is a program to help dads love and lead their families well. We provide practical resources to dads through events in NFL stadiums, dads and kids breakfast programs, and online at allprodad.com.

 iMOM is a program to help moms love and nurture their families well. Being a mom is hard! We inspire and encourage moms to be the best they can be by providing resources that help online at imom.com.

 The Family Minute with Mark Merrill is a daily radio feature that offers advice on marriage, parenting and family relationships. The Family Minute is heard on over 350 radio stations in 46 states and globally on American Forces Network.
